I0480381

ART BOOKS

FROM CRESCENT MOON PUBLISHING

Leonardo da Vinci
by James Pearson

Early Netherlandish Painting
by Rosalind Mutter

Piero della Francesca
by Naomi Haskell

Giovanni Bellini
by Julia Davis

Eric Gill: Nuptials of God
by Anthony Hoyland

Minimal Art and Artists In the 1960s and After
by Laura Garrard

Postwar Art
by George Knighton

Vincent van Gogh: Visionary Landscapes
by Stuart Morris

Max Beckmann
by Stuart Morris

Egon Schiele: Sex and Death in Purple Stockings
by D. Simon Eade

Mark Rothko: The Art of Transcendence
by Julia Davis

Jasper Johns
by L.M. Poole

Brice Marden
by Laura Garrard

Frank Stella: American Abstract Artist
by James Pearson

FRA ANGELICO

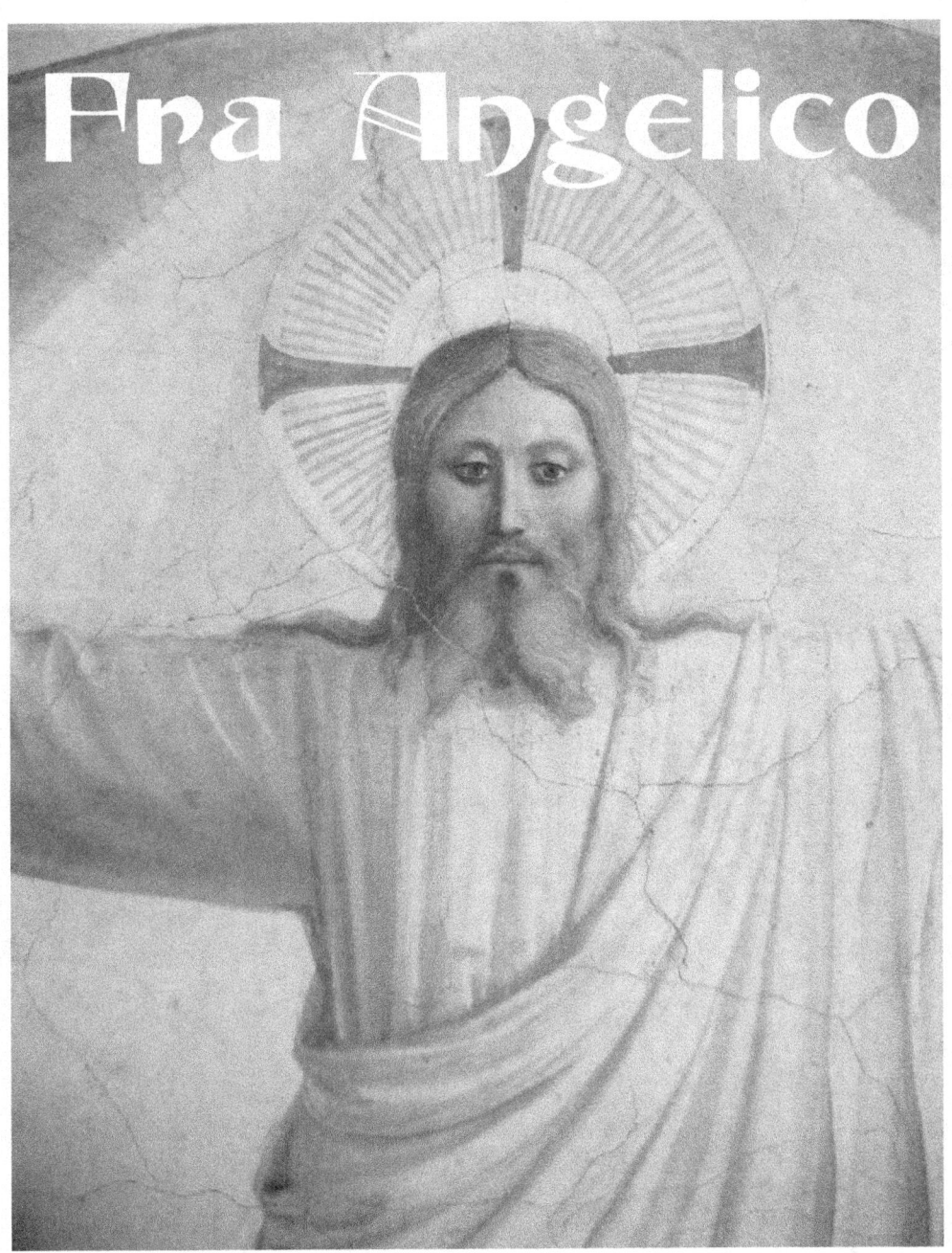

Fra Angelico

JAMES MASON

Crescent Moon

First published 1902. This edition © 2017.

Printed and bound in the U.S.A.
Set in Book Antiqua 10 on 14pt.
Designed by Radiance Graphics.

All rights reserved. No part of this book may be reprinted or reproduced, stored in a retrieval system, or transmitted, in any form or by any means, electronic, mechanical, photocopying, recording or otherwise, without permission from the publisher.

Images are used for information and research purposes, with no infringement of copyright or rights intended.

Thanks to the authors and publishers quoted.

British Library Cataloguing in Publication data

ISBN-13 9781861716019 (Pbk)

CRESCENT MOON PUBLISHING
P.O. Box 1312, Maidstone, Kent, ME14 5XU
Great Britain, www.crmoon.com

CONTENTS

NOTE ON THE TEXT

The text is from *Fra Angelico* by James Mason, published by
T.C. & E.C. Jack, London and Frederick A. Stokes, New York,
1902, as part of the Masterpieces In Colour series, edited by T.
Leman Hare.

The illustrations discussed in the book are included in the
illustrations section, along with many other works, including
Angelico's contemporaries.

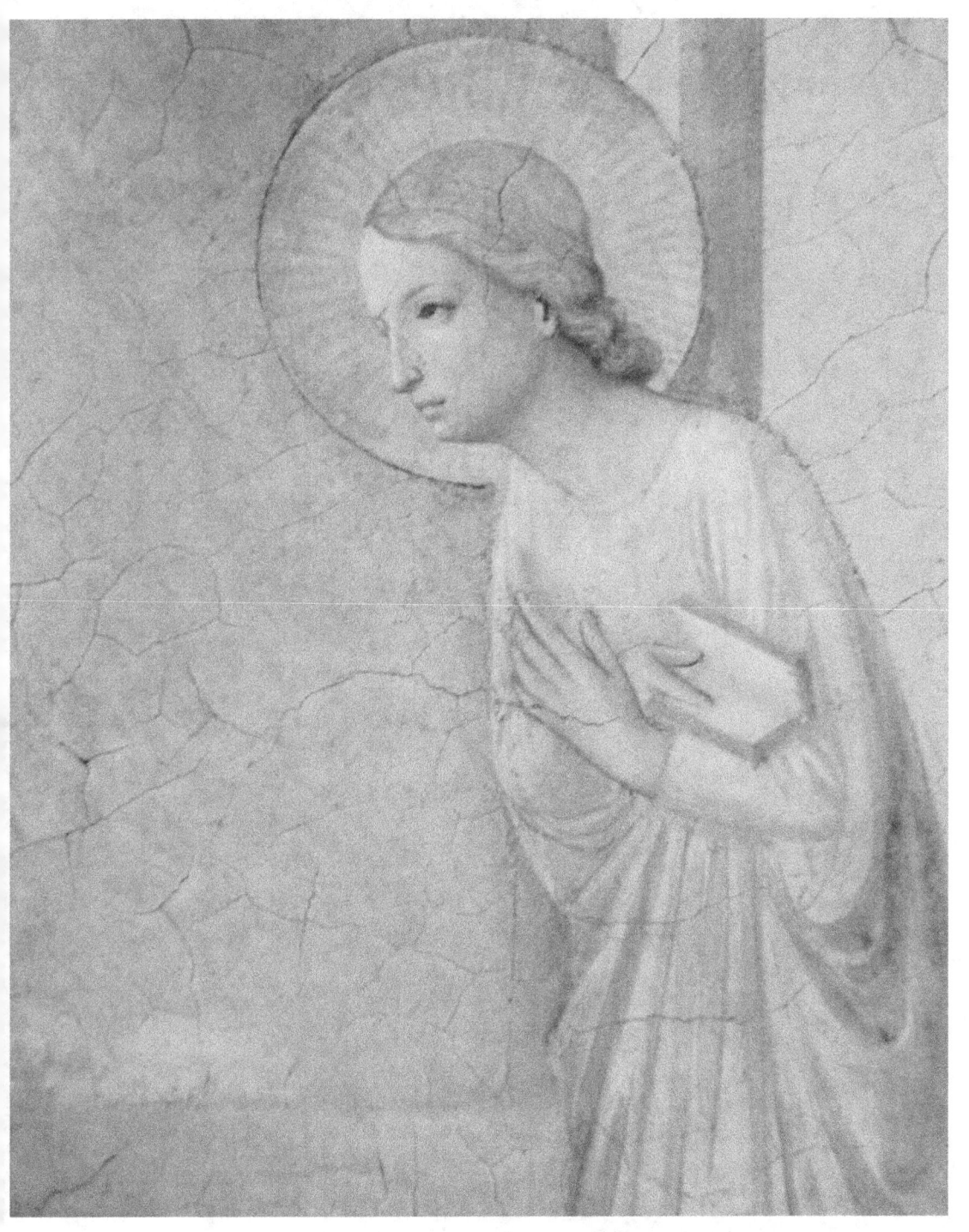

Fra Angelico, Annunciation, cell 3 at San Marco

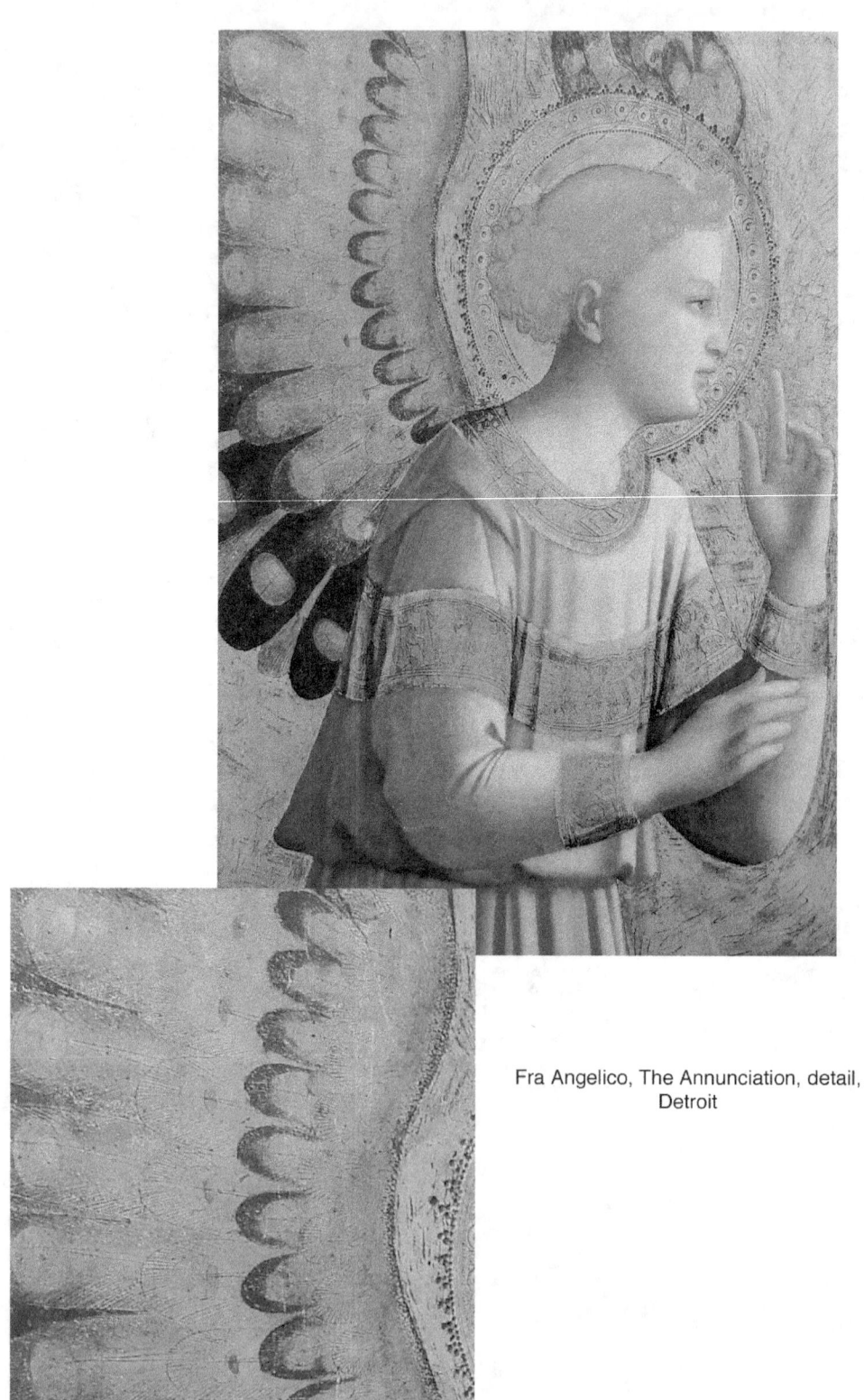

Fra Angelico, The Annunciation, detail,
Detroit

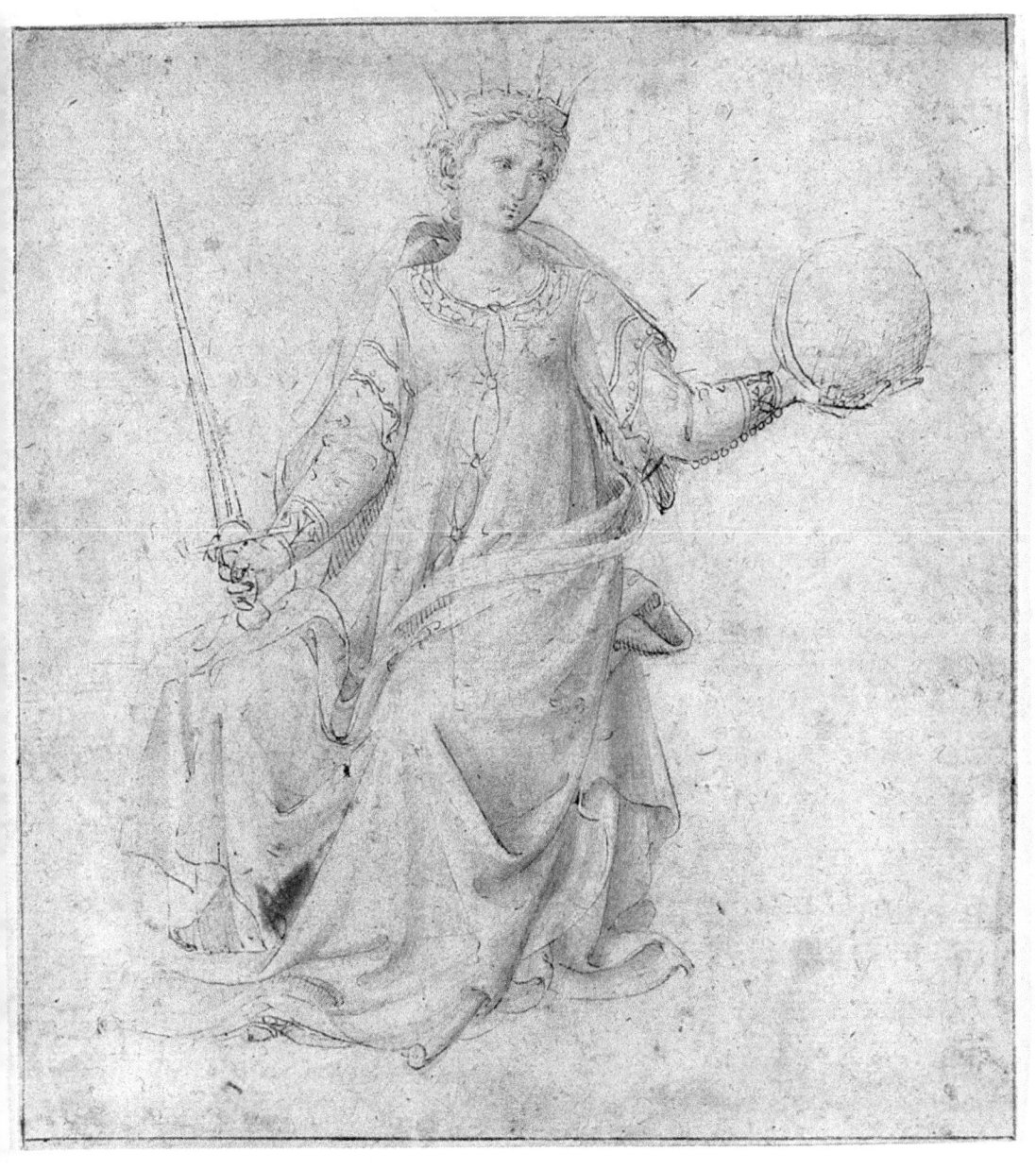

Fra Angelico, Justice, Metropolitan Museum of Art, NYC

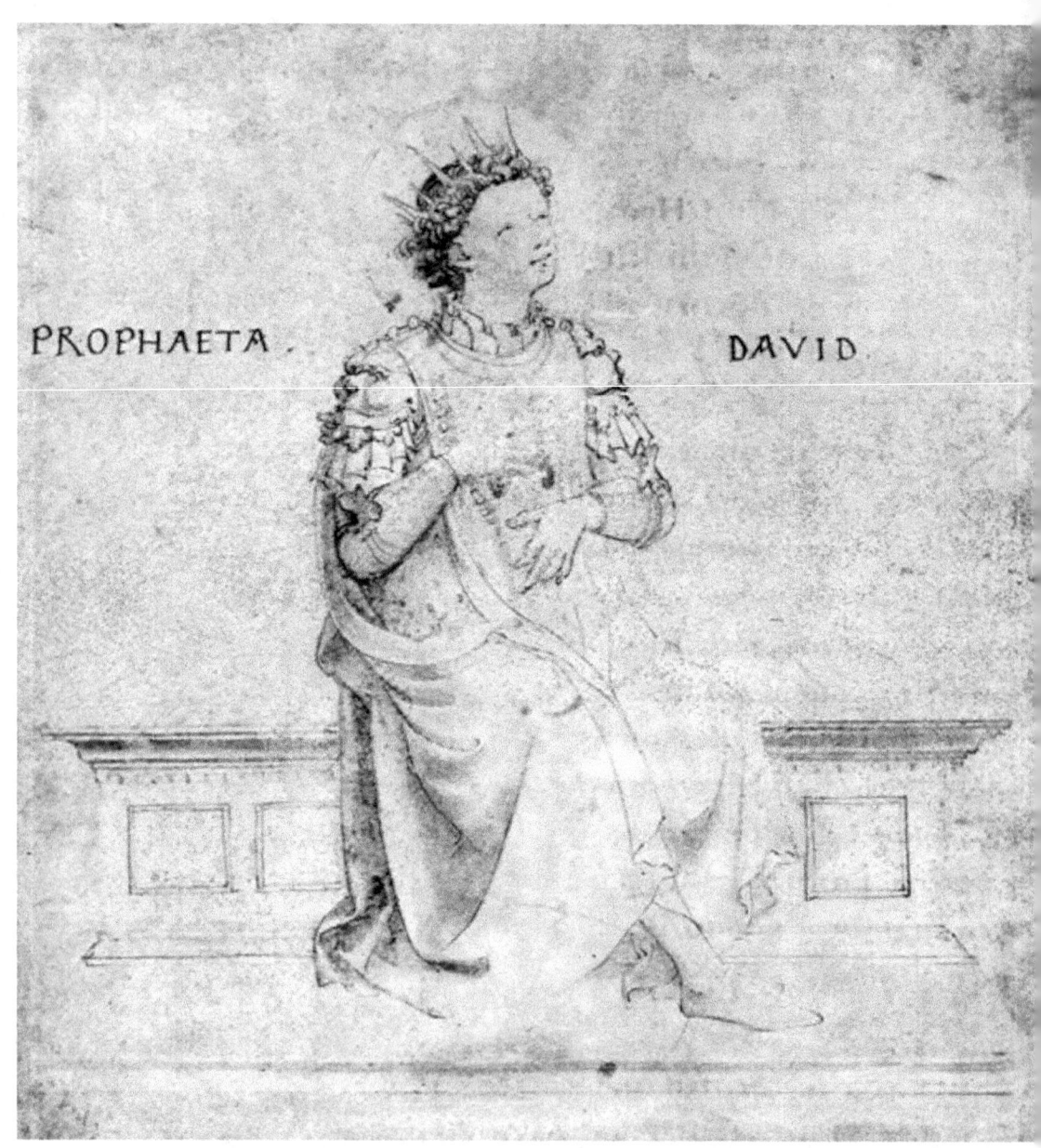

PROPHAETA.　　　　　DAVID.

Fra Angelico, King David, 1430, San Marco

I

INTRODUCTION

ROUND the peaceful life and delicately imaginative work of Guido da Vicchio, the Florentine artist who is known to the world at large as Fra Angelico, critics and laymen continue to wage a fierce controversy.

While few are heard to deny the merit of the artist's exquisite achievement, it is hard to find, even among those who are interested in early Florentine religion and art, men who can agree about Fra Angelico's positions between the monastery and the studio. "He was a man with a beautiful mind," says one; "a light of the Church, a saint by temperament, and he chanced to be a painter." "You are entirely wrong," says the supporter of the opposing theory; "he was a Heaven-sent artist who chanced to take the vows."

So the schools of art and theology rage furiously together, after the fashion of the two men who approached a statue from opposite sides and quarrelled because one said that the shield carried by the bronze figure was made of gold, and the other said it was made of silver. Incensed by each other's obstinacy they drew swords and fought until they both fell helpless to the ground, only to be assured by a third traveller, who chanced to pass by, that the shield had gold on one side and silver on the other.

Standing well apart from the enthusiasts of both sides, the average man sees that Fra Angelico was an artist of remarkable attainments and at the same time a devout, God-fearing friar, who seems to have deserved a great part at least of the praise he received from the honeyed pen of Giorgio Vasari. Naturally enough the modern artist finds in Fra Angelico, or "Beato" Angelico as he is sometimes called, one of the most interesting painters of the fifteenth century, and he does not bother about the fact that his hero chanced to be a Dominican brother. Very devout Catholics, on the other hand, will approach Fra Angelico's work on the literary side, and will be profoundly conscious of the fact that he was the first great artist of Italy who, realising the maternity of the Madonna, represented her as a mother full of human affection, and the Holy Child as a beautiful baby boy. It is the painter's abiding claim to our regard that he brought life to his walls and panels, that they present the living, palpitating sentiment of men and women and children, that he painted for us the flowers that blossomed round him and the countryside through which he wandered in his hours of ease. The technical achievement, the gradual but steady improvement in dealing with composition and masses of colour, the extraordinary change from the stiff early figures to the supple ones of the later years, the splendid growth of the artistic sense, from all these things the devotee turns aside. He is not unconscious of the change, for the results achieved by the painter account for the spectator's riper and fuller appreciation, but he cannot analyse it. Of far more moment to him is the thought that all Fra Angelico's life and art were given to the service of the Church, that he laboured without ceasing to present the Gospel stories in the most attractive form, despising the material rewards that awaited such achievements as his. Ease, luxury and the praise of the world at large the Dominican dismissed with fine indifference, believing that his reward would come when his task was ended, and the work of his hands should praise him in the gates. "Here," his orthodox latter-day admirers say, "is the man of noble convictions and pure life, who stood for all that was best in religion. As he chanced to have the gifts of a painter, he used those gifts to develop his mission. Painting with him was no more than a means to an end, and that end was the glorification of God." The dispute must needs be endless; for we cannot see through the four centuries that separate us from the artist, and every man takes from a picture some echo of what he brought to it.

In sober truth the matter is of far less importance than the makers of controversy imagine. It should suffice both parties to agree that Fra Angelico was a great painter and a great man, that his association with the Church afforded him the opportunity of leaving behind him work that has a spiritual as well as artistic quality. His altar-pieces and frescoes seem to breathe the serene atmosphere of an age of faith; they tell of a quiet retired life amid surroundings that remain unrivalled to-day, even though our horizon is widened and we know the New World as well as the Old.

There are examples of the painter's art in the National Gallery and in the Louvre, in Rome and in Perugia; but Florence holds by far the greatest number. In Florence we find the series painted to decorate the "Silver Press" of the Annunziata, and more than a dozen other works of importance. The Uffizi guards the famous "Madonna dei Linajuoli" and the "Coronation of the Virgin" from Santa Maria Nuova. The Convent of San Marco, to which the Brotherhood of San Dominico went in 1346 from Fiesole, holds the famous frescoes in cloister, chapter-house, and cells, and offers an illuminating guide to the painter's ideals and intentions, in work that is the ripe product of middle age. So it is to Florence that one must go to study the painter, though there are one or two works from his hands in Fiesole across the valley, while the collection in Perugia is not to be overlooked, and Rome holds some of the best work of the artist's hand, painted in the closing years. For all the surging waves of tourists that break upon Florence, month in, month out, filling streets and galleries with discordant noises, and giving them an air of unrest strangely out of keeping with their traditional aspect, the city preserves sufficient of its old-time character to enable the student to study Fra Angelico's pictures in an atmosphere that would not have been altogether repugnant to the artist himself. Save in seasons when the city is full to overflowing the Convent of San Marco receives few visitors, while in the Academy and at the Uffizi there are so many expressions of a more flamboyant art that there is seldom any lack of space round the panels Angelico painted.

There are some days when San Marco is altogether free from visitors, and then the frescoed cells, through which the great white glare of the day steals softly and subdued, seem to be waiting for the devotees who will return no more, and one looks anxiously to cloisters, and garden and chapter-house for some signs of the life that rose so far above the varied emptiness of our own.

II

THE PAINTER'S EARLY DAYS

When Guido da Vicchio was born in the little fortified town from which he takes his name, the town that looks out upon the Apennines on the North and West, and towards Monte Giovo on the South, the Medici family was just beginning to raise its head in Florence. Salvestro di Medici had originated the "Tumult of the Ciompi"; the era of democratic government in the city was drawing to a close. Beyond the boundaries of Florence the various states into which Italy was divided were quarrelling violently among themselves. The throne of St. Peter was rent by schism, Pope and anti-Pope were striving one against the other in fashion that was amazing and calculated to bring the Papal power into permanent disrepute. It was a period of uncertainty and unrest, prolific in saints and sinners, voluptuaries and ascetics. No student of history will need to be reminded that it is to periods such as this that the world has learned to look for its remarkable men.

Doubtless some echo of the surrounding strife penetrated beyond the walls of Vicchio when Guido was a little boy, for he lived in a fortified town built for purposes of war. It is not unreasonable to suppose that he may have seen enough of the stress and strife peculiar to the age to have turned his thoughts to other things. If a lad, born with a peaceable and affectionate disposition, be brought into contact with violence at an early age, his peaceful tendencies will be strengthened, he will avoid all sources and scenes of strife. We know nothing of the painter's boyhood, but, looking round at the conditions prevailing in Florence, it seems more than likely that the years were not quite restful.

In the absence of authentic information one may do no more than suggest that, when the lad was newly in his teens, he served in the studio of some local painter and discovered his own talent. Attempts have been made to give the teacher a name and a history, but these efforts, for all that they are interesting, lack authenticity. Far away in Florence the first faint light of the Revival of Learning was shining upon the more intelligent partisans of all the jarring factions. The claims of the religious life were being put forward with extraordinary fervour and ability by a great teacher and preacher, John the Dominican, who appears to have reformed the somewhat lax rules of his order. We are told that he travelled on foot from town to town after the fashion of his time, calling upon sinners to repent, and summoning to join the brotherhood all those who regarded life as a dangerous and uncertain road to a greater and nobler future. Clerics looked askance at the signs of the times, for although art and literature were coming into favour, although Florence was becoming the centre of a great humanist movement, the change was associated with a recrudescence of pagan luxury and vices that boded ill for the maintenance of moral law.

Perhaps John the Dominican preached in Vicchio, perhaps Guido and his younger brother Benedetto heard him elsewhere, but wherever the message was delivered it went home, for it is recorded that in the year 1407, when Fra Angelico would have been just twenty years old, he and Benedetto travelled to the Dominican Convent on the hillside at Fiesole and applied for admission to the order. The brothers were welcomed and sent to serve their novitiate at Cortona, where some of Fra Angelico's earliest known work was painted. They returned to Fiesole in the following year, but the Dominican establishment there was soon broken up because the Florentines had acknowledged Alexander V. as Pope, and the Dominican Brotherhood supported his opponent, Gregory XI. Foligno and Cortona were visited in turn. In the former city the Church of the Dominicans remains to-day; and so the brethren sought peace beyond Fiesole, until in 1418 the Council of Constance healed the wounds of Mother Church. Then Pope Martin V. came to live in Florence, where John XXIII. paid him obeisance, and the Dominican friars returned to their hillside home beyond the city, that was then, according to the historian Bisticci, "in a most blissful state, abounding in excellent men in every faculty, and full of admirable citizens."

And now Fra Angelico, as he must be called in future, settled down to his first important work. He had learned as much as his associates could teach him, and had gathered sufficient strength of purpose, intelligence and judgment, to enable him to deal with the problems of his art as he thought best. It may be said that Fra Angelico built the bridge by which mediæval art travelled into the country of the Renaissance. Indeed, he did more than this, for having built the bridge, he boldly passed over it in the last years of his life. We can see in his work the unmistakable marks of the years of his labour. He started out equipped with the heavy burden of all the conventions of mediævalism. Against that drawback he could set independence of thought, and a goodly measure of that Florentine restlessness that led men to express themselves in every art-form known to the world. No Florentine artist of the Quattrocento held that painting was enough if he could add sculpture to it, or that sculpture would serve if architecture could be added to that. Had there been any other form of art-expression to their hands, the Florentines would have used it, because they were as men who seek to speak in many languages. This restlessness, this prodigality of effort, was to find its final expression in Leonardo da Vinci, who entered the world as the Dominican friar was leaving it.

In the early days Fra Angelico must have been a miniaturist. Vasari speaks of him as being pre-eminent as painter, miniaturist, and religious man, and the painting of miniatures cramped the painter's style in fashion that detracts from the merits of the earlier pictures, but of course Fra Angelico is by no means the only artist to whom miniature painting has been a pitfall.

Professor Langton Douglas has pointed out, in his admirable and exhaustive work on Fra Angelico, that the artist was profoundly influenced by the great painters and architects of his time, and has even used this undisputed fact as an aid to ascertain the approximate date of certain pictures. We can hardly wonder that the influence should be felt by a sensitive artist, who responded readily to outside forces, when we consider the quality of the work that sculpture and architecture were giving to the world in those early days of the Quattrocento. Men of genius dominated every path in life and Florence held far more than a fair share of them.

Among the works belonging to the years before Fra Angelico went to San Marco, and painted the frescoes that stand for his middle period at its best, are the Altar-piece at Cortona, "The Annunciation" and "The Last Judgment," in the Academy of Florence, and the famous "Madonna da Linajuoli," with its twelve angels playing divers musical instruments on the frame round the central panel. These angels have made the Madonna of the Flax-workers the best known of all the painter's works. So long the delight of the public eye they are very harshly criticised to-day, and not without reason, for doubtless they are flat and stiff productions enough. But they have a certain naïve beauty of their own, and because they have done more than work of far greater merit to spread the fame of Fra Angelico, because they have been the source of great delight to countless people despised and rejected of art critics, it has seemed reasonable to present some of them in this little volume, side by side with those more important works of the master to which so many artists of the Renaissance are indebted. We may rest assured that to the painter the angels were very real angels indeed, the best that his art and devotion could express.

Other important works of this first period, which may be taken to range from 1407 to 1435, are the altar-pieces known as the Madonna of Cortona, the Madonna of Perugia, and the Madonna of the Annelena, the last-named being in the Academy at Florence. Critics and artists can divide the painter's life into four or more divisions expressed to them by changes in his style; but a simpler division suffices here.

Looking at Fra Angelico with eyes that the nineteenth century has trained, we speak of this early work as of less importance than what followed, but in so doing it is quite easy to speak or write as several of his critics have done in very unreasonable fashion. Certainly the artist, who in the last years of his life painted the picture of St. Lorenzo distributing alms, and the scenes in the life of St. Stephen, has travelled very far from the painter of the "Last Judgment" that may be seen in Florence; but, even in the early days of Cortona, Fra Angelico was a modern of the moderns. He was a man who worked and thought far in advance of his times, who had the wide outlook that we have learned to associate with all the Florentine artists of the Quattrocento, and he left the boundaries of the painter's art far wider than he found them. Doubtless many of his contemporaries found his work daring and even immoral in so far as it departed from the traditions that had satisfied his predecessors. He had an individuality that expressed itself in fashion unmistakable before he was thirty years of age, and developed steadily down to the last year of his life. Divorced by his calling from the cares and joys of other men, he responded with delight to the larger and more general aspects of life. Fra Angelico had a keen and eager eye for natural beauty; he seems to have gone to the countryside for all the inspiration that remained to seek when the sacred writings were laid aside. The maternal aspect with which he endowed the Madonna, who had hitherto been as stiff and formless as though carved out of wood, testifies to the artist's recognition of maternity as he saw it among

▼ 23

the simple peasants his order served. He restored humanity to Mother and Child. The child-like Christ, no longer a doll but a real *bambino*, tells us how deeply the painter entered into the spirit of a life that the rules of his order forbade him to share. Just as some women who do not marry seem to keep for the world at large the measure of loving sympathy that would have been concentrated upon their children; so this painter monk, who had paid his vows to poverty, chastity, and obedience, could express upon his canvas the affection and the sentiment that would have been bestowed under other circumstances upon a chosen helpmate. Lacking the joys of healthy domesticity he turned to Nature with a loving eye and an intelligence that cannot be over-estimated and, if he knew hours wherein, manlike, he mourned for the life forbidden, the consolation was at hand. The Earth Mother consoled him. In his earliest canvases he expresses his love of flowers, the love of a child for the sights that make the earliest appeal to our sense of beauty. His angels are set in flowering fields, they carry blossoms that bloom in the fields beyond Cortona, and upon the hillside of Fiesole. Clearly the painter saw Paradise around him. Roses and pinks seem to be his favourite flowers, he paints them with a loving care, knowing them in bud and in full leaf and, just as he went to Nature for the decorative side of his art, so in a way he may be said to have gone to Nature in her brightest and most joyous moods for his colours. His palette seems to have borrowed its glory from the rainbow – the gold, the green, the blue, and the red are surely as bright and clear in his pictures as they are in the great and gleaming arch that Easterns call in their own picturesque fashion "The Bride of the Rain."

In all his work Fra Angelico showed himself an innovator, a man who, in thinking for himself, would not allow his own clear vision to be obscured by the conventions that bound men of smaller mentality and less significant achievement. At the same time he was very observant of the progress of his peers, particularly in architecture, and students of this branch of art cannot fail to notice his response to the developments brought about by Michelozzo and Brunelleschi. Even in the first period of his art he would have seemed a daring innovator to his contemporaries for, all unconsciously he was taking his share in shaping the great Renaissance movement that left so many timid souls outside the radius of its illumination.

In the early days he approached the human body with some diffidence, and though a greater courage in this regard is the keynote of Renaissance painting, the earlier timidity is hardly to be wondered at when we consider the attitude of the religious houses towards humanity in its physical aspect, and how necessary it was to avoid anything approaching sensuous imagery throughout that anxious period of transition. As he grew older and more confident of his powers, Fra Angelico seems to have freed himself from some of the restrictions that beset an artist who is also a religious. He, too, learned to glorify the human form.

His love for Nature remained constant throughout all the years of his life; he was sufficiently daring to introduce real landscape into his pictures, and by so doing, to become one of the fathers of landscape painting. His angels have a setting in the Italy he knew best, the flowers that strew their paths are those he may have gathered in the convent garden; for even his vivid and exalted imagination could not create aught more beautiful than those that grew so freely and wild by the wayside, or were tended by his brethren in San Marco.

We find throughout the pictures a suggestion that the life of the artist was a serene and tranquil one that, while he was actively concerned with things of art throughout the district he knew best, he was sheltered by the house of the brotherhood from the tumult and turmoil that beset Fiesole, Cortona, and Foligno in the days of his youth. When he went to San Marco in Florence, where his most enduring memorial remains to this day, Fra Angelico was a man of experience and an independence so far in advance of his time, that some of the work he had accomplished comes to us to-day with a suggestion of absolute modernity in thought if not in treatment. No beauty that our more sophisticated age can reveal to us had passed him by, he paints Nature as Milton painted it when he wrote the "Masque of Comus" and "l'Allegro." And this manner of painting, so different from that of men who mix themselves with the world and surrender to its fascinations, is the painting that endures.

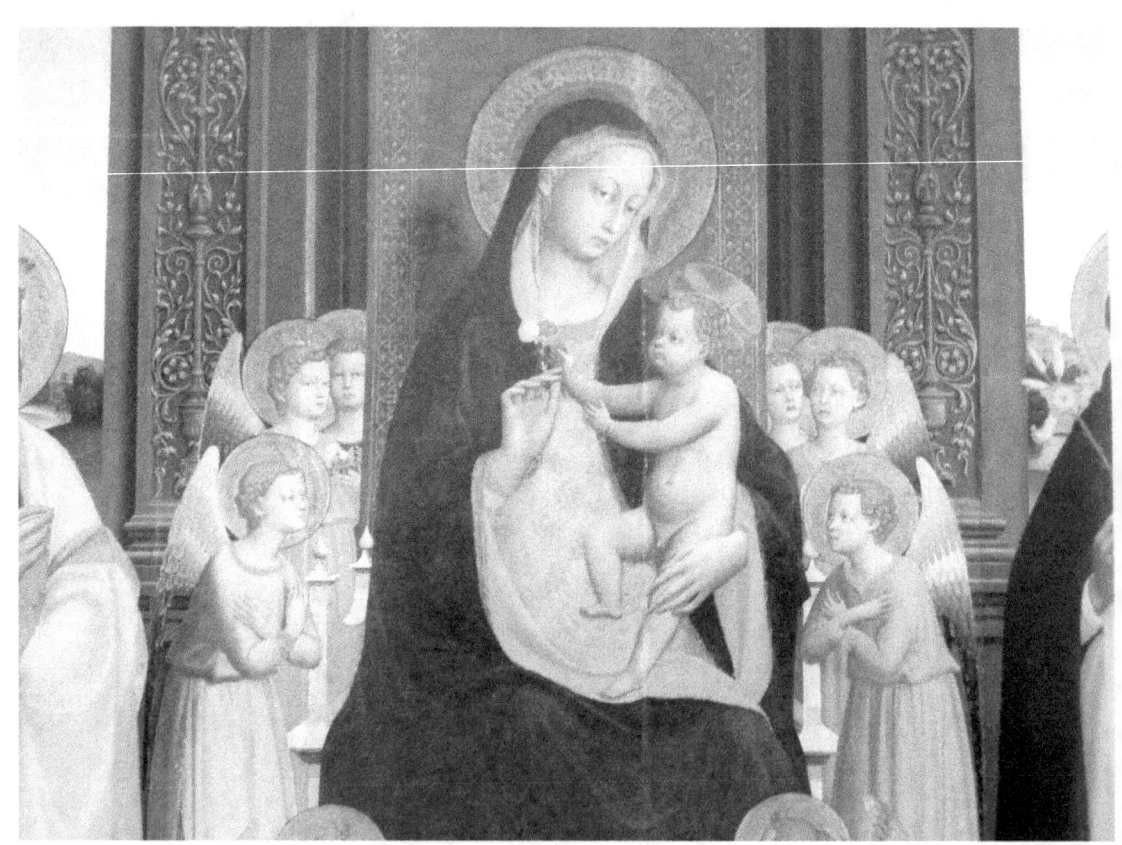

Fra Angelico, Virgin and Child, Fiesole

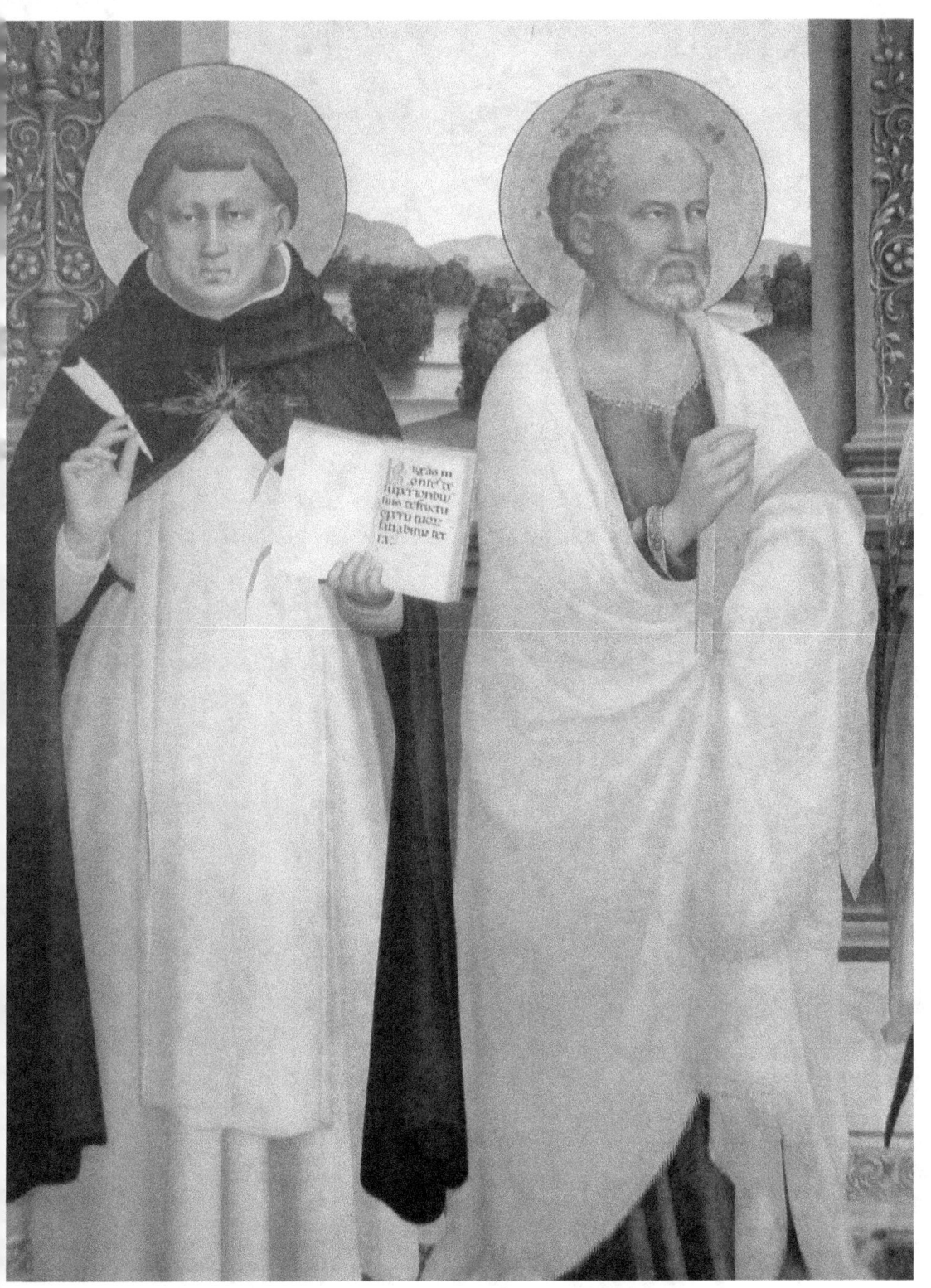

Fra Angelico, Virgin and Child Enthroned, c. 1424-25, detail, Fiesole

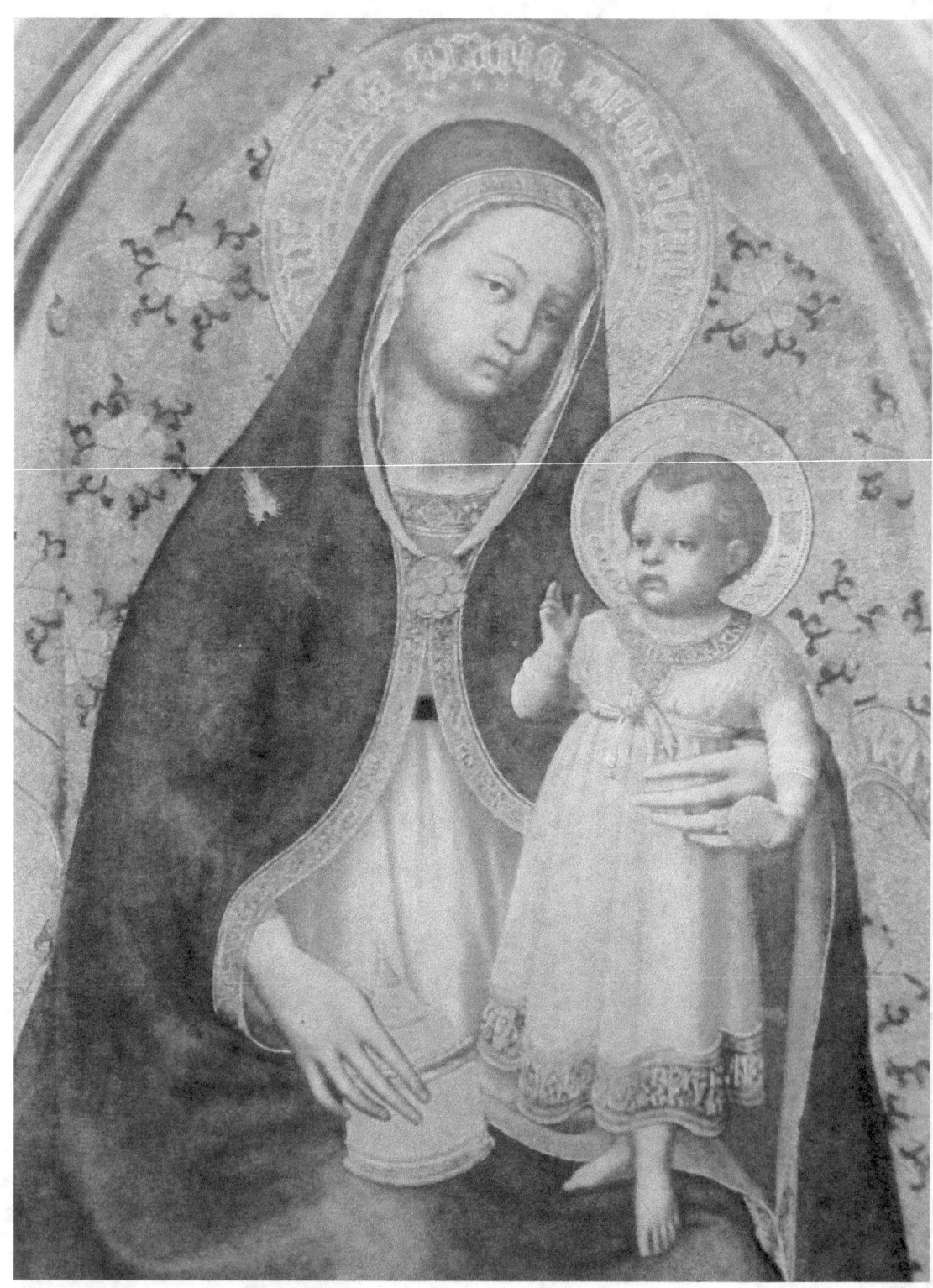

Fra Angelico, San Pier Martire Altarpiece

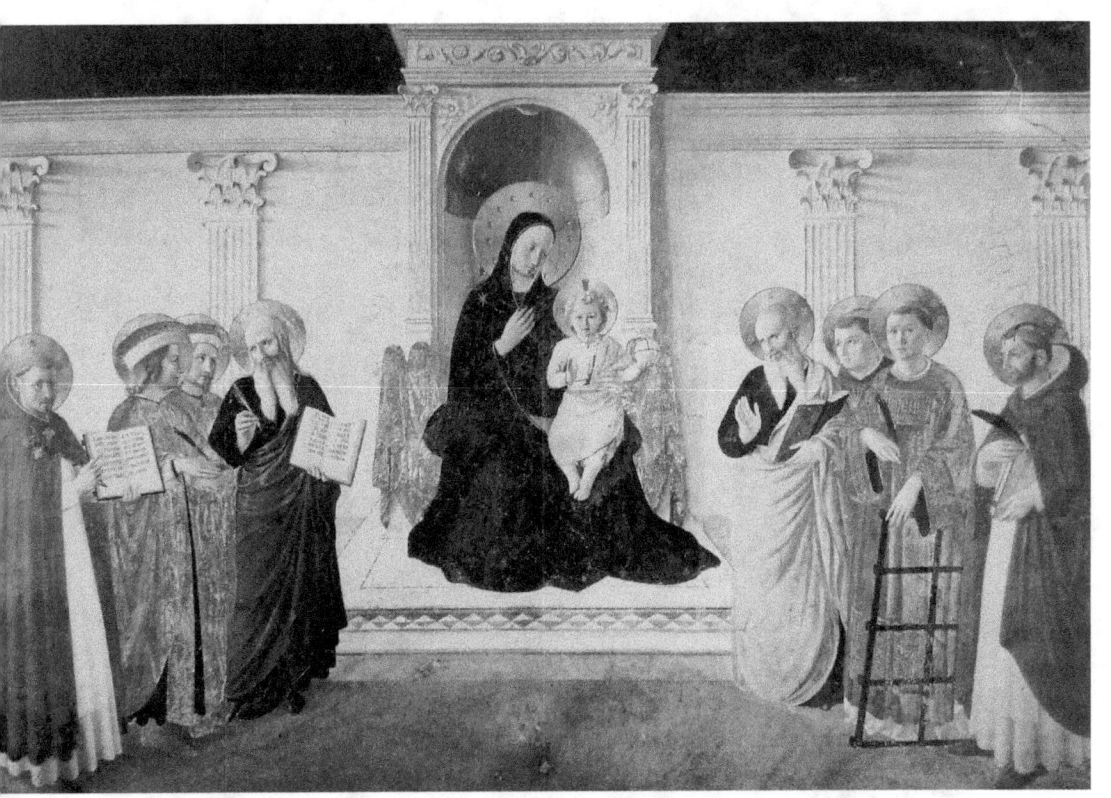

Fra Angelico, Sacra Conversazione, 1440

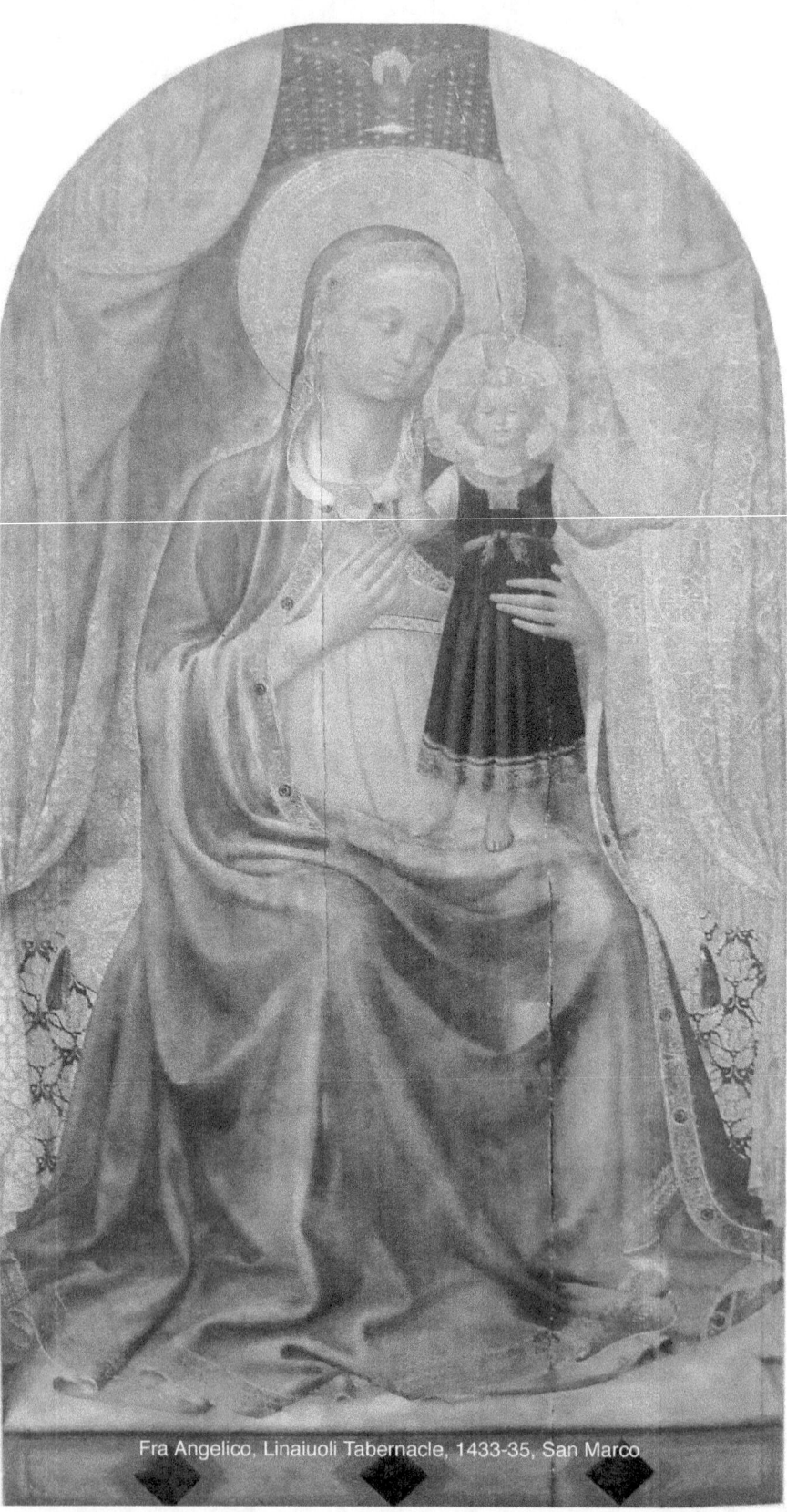

Fra Angelico, Linaiuoli Tabernacle, 1433-35, San Marco

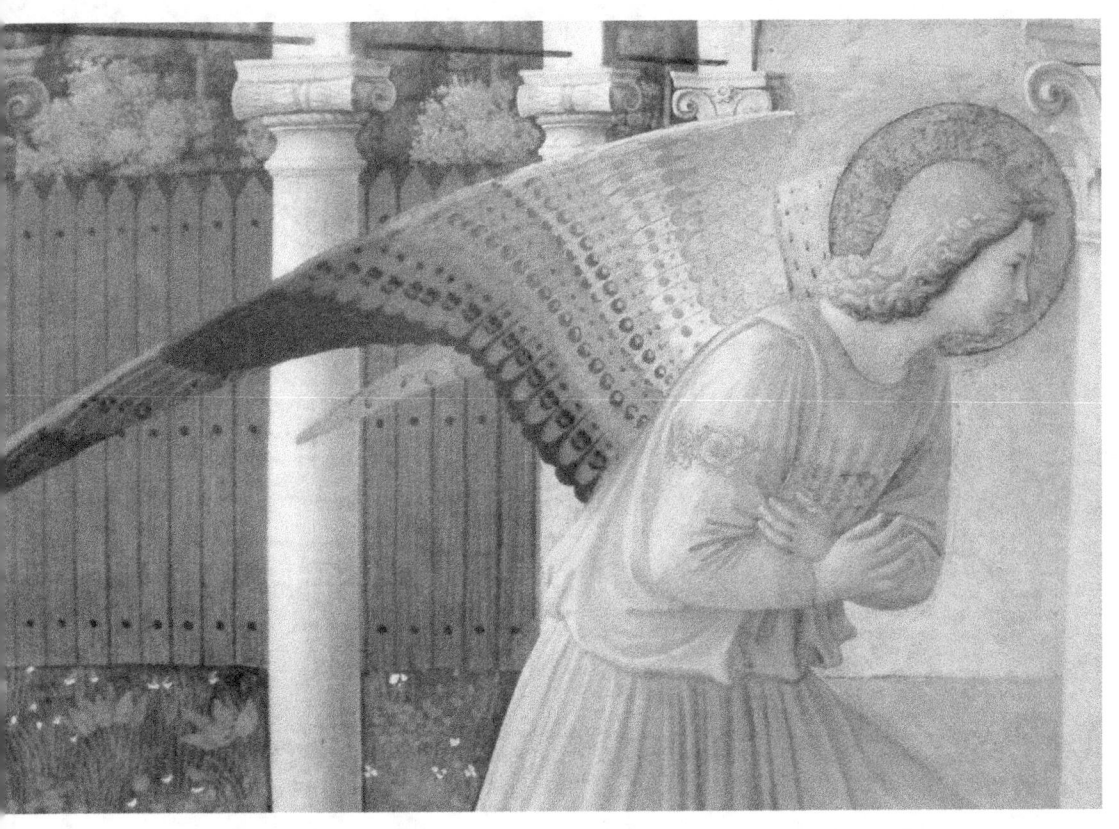

Fra Angelico, Annunciation, c. 1450, detail, upper corridor, San Marco

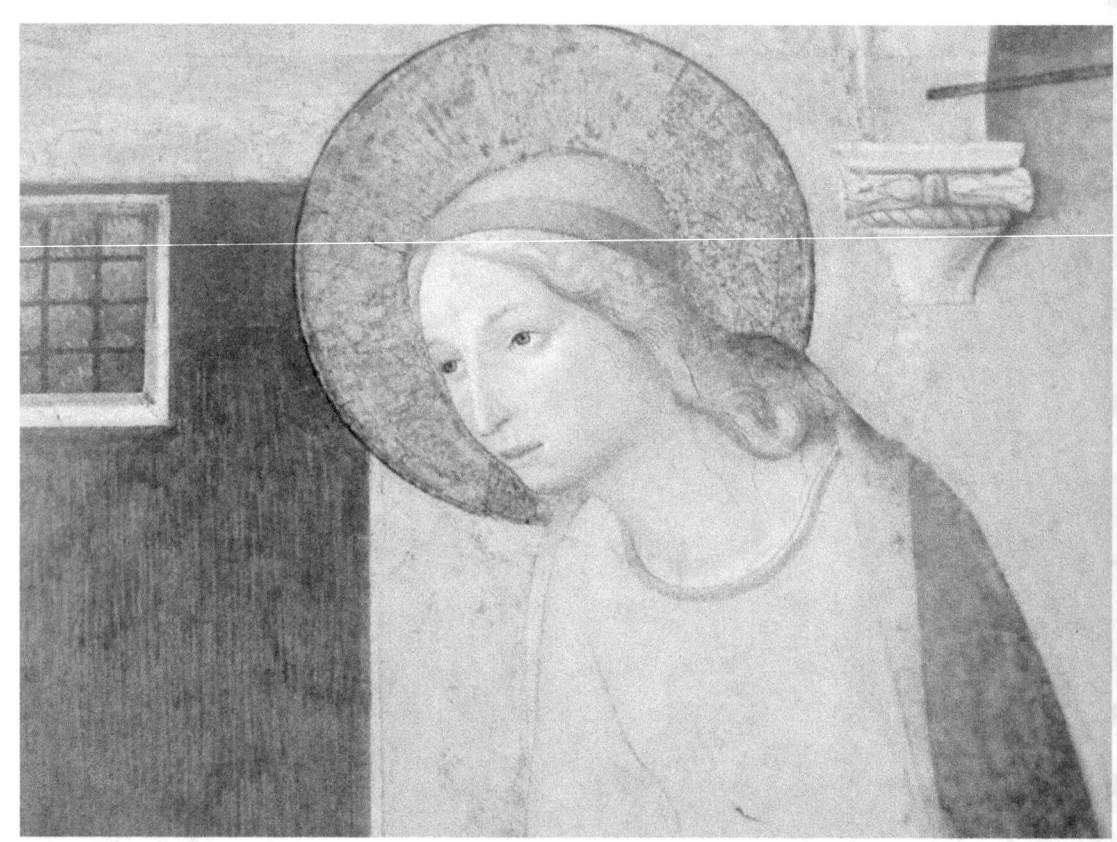

Fra Angelico, Annunciation, detail, San Marco, Florence

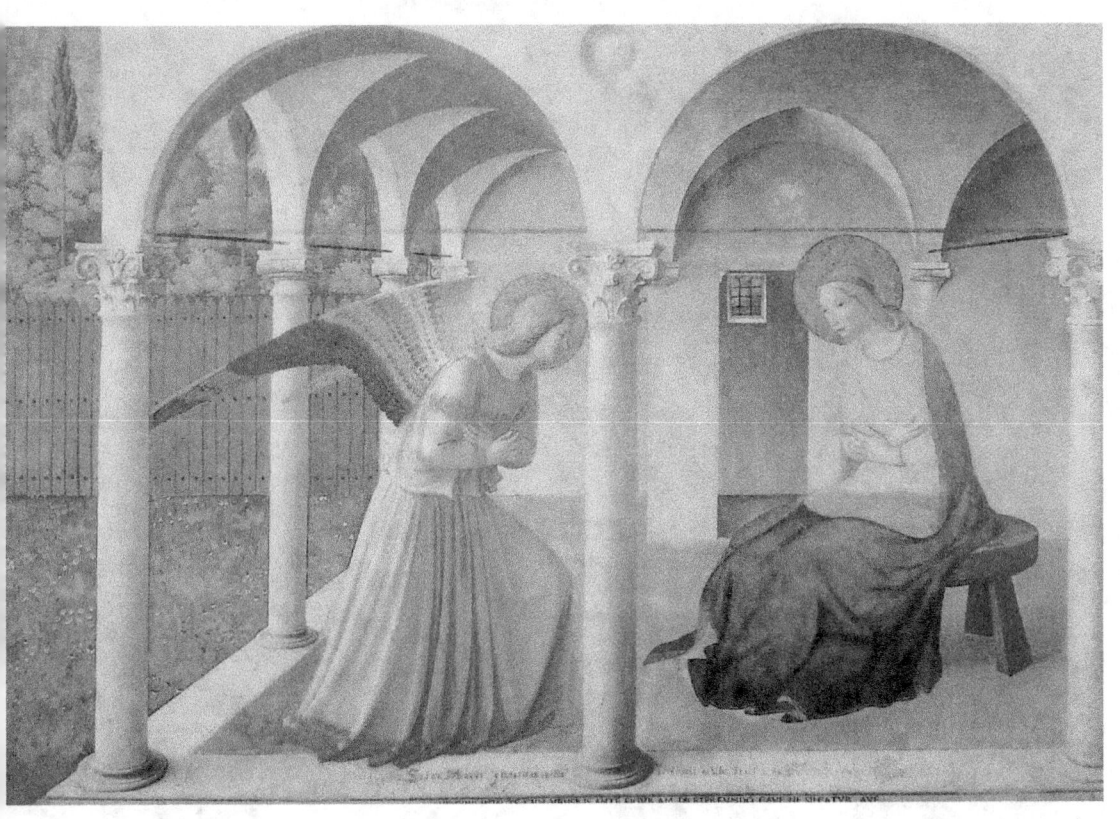

Fra Angelico, The Annunciation, San Marco, Florence

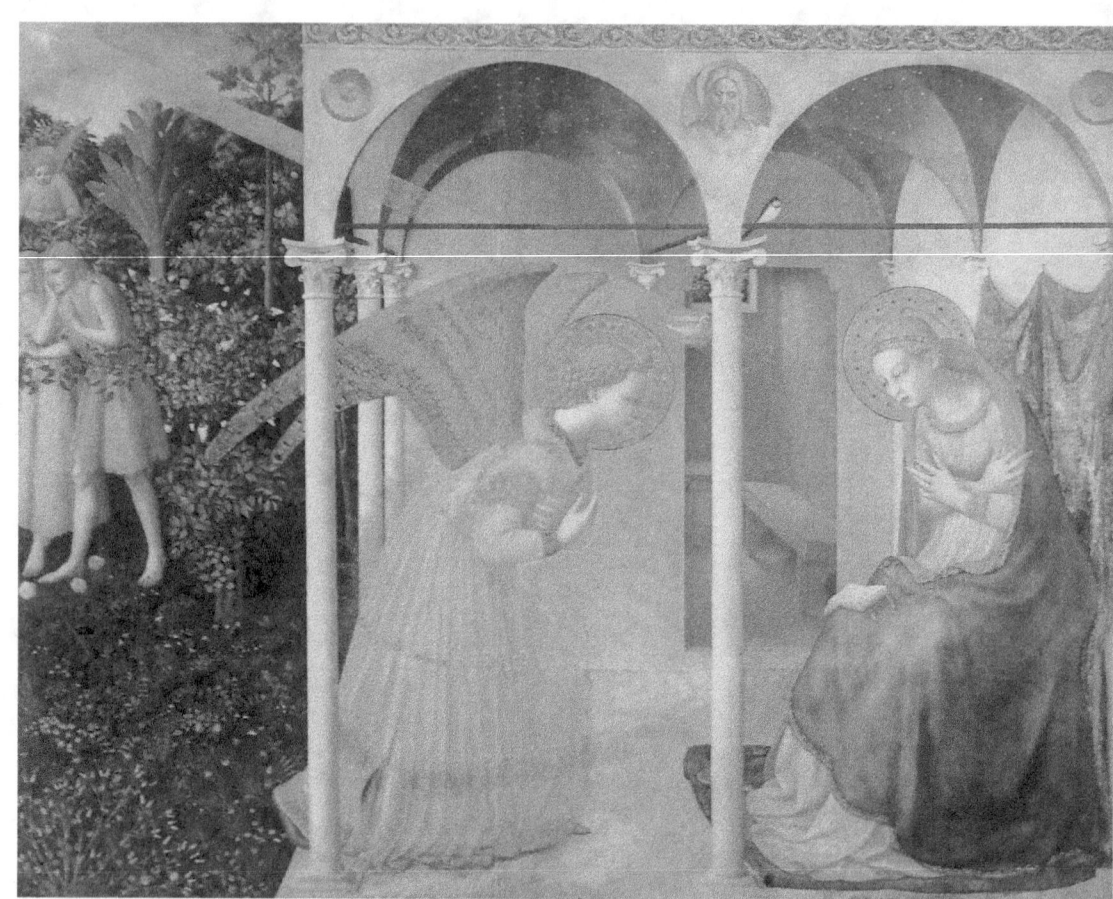

Fra Angelico, Annunciation, Prado, Madrid

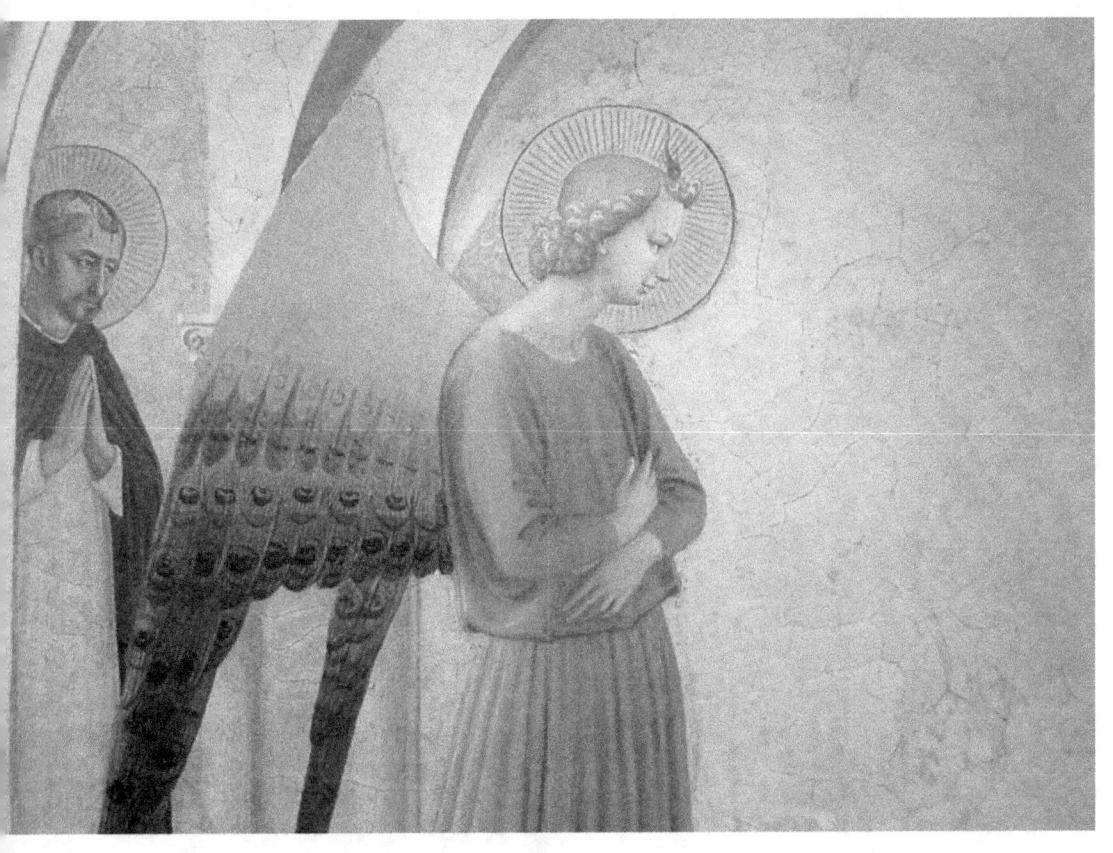

Fra Angelico, Annunciation, cell 3, San Marco

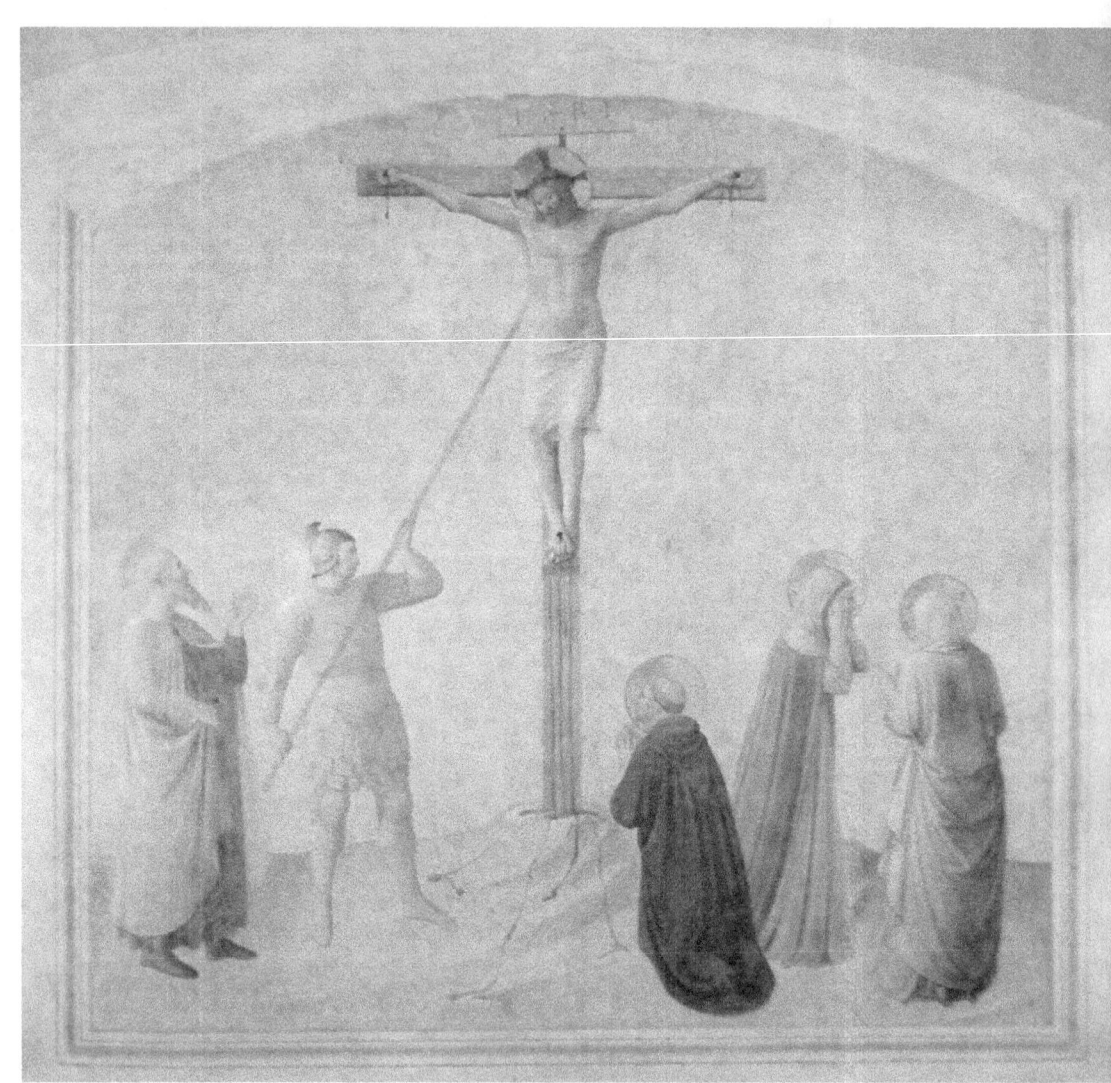

Fra Angelico, Crucifixion, cell 42, San Marco

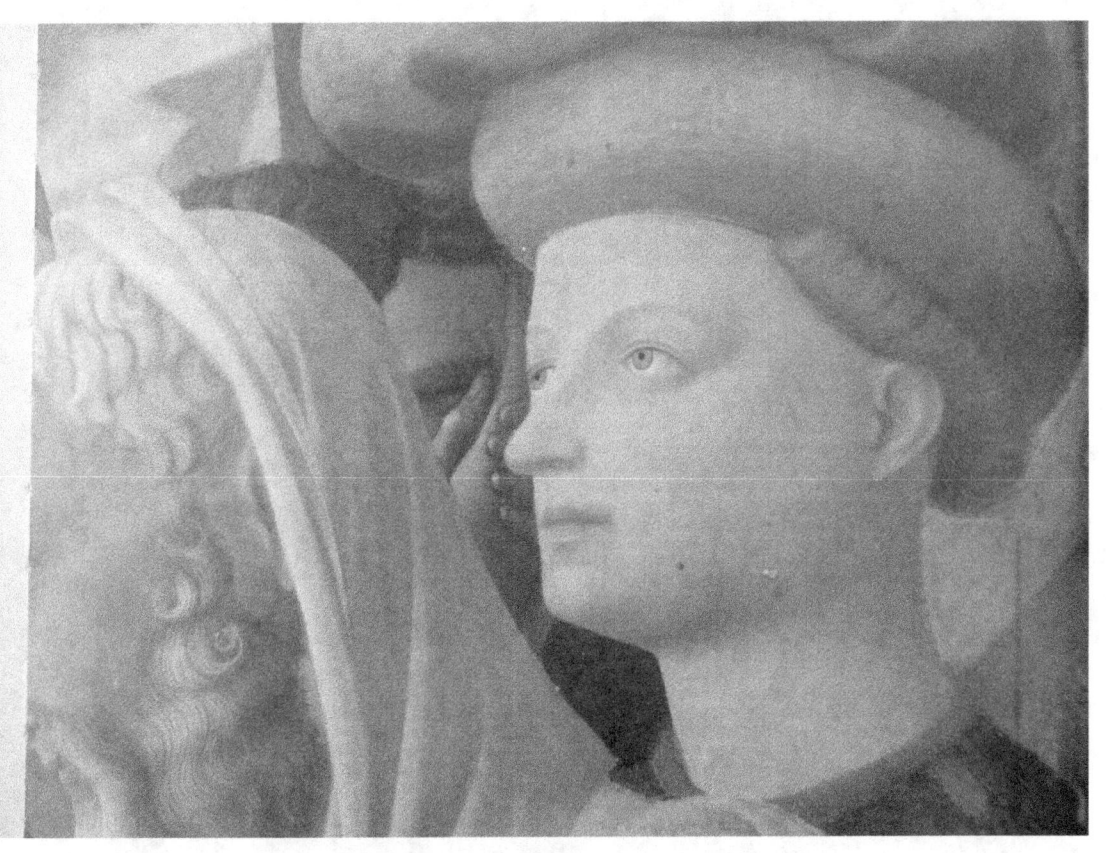

Fra Angelico, Descent From the Cross, detail, San Marco

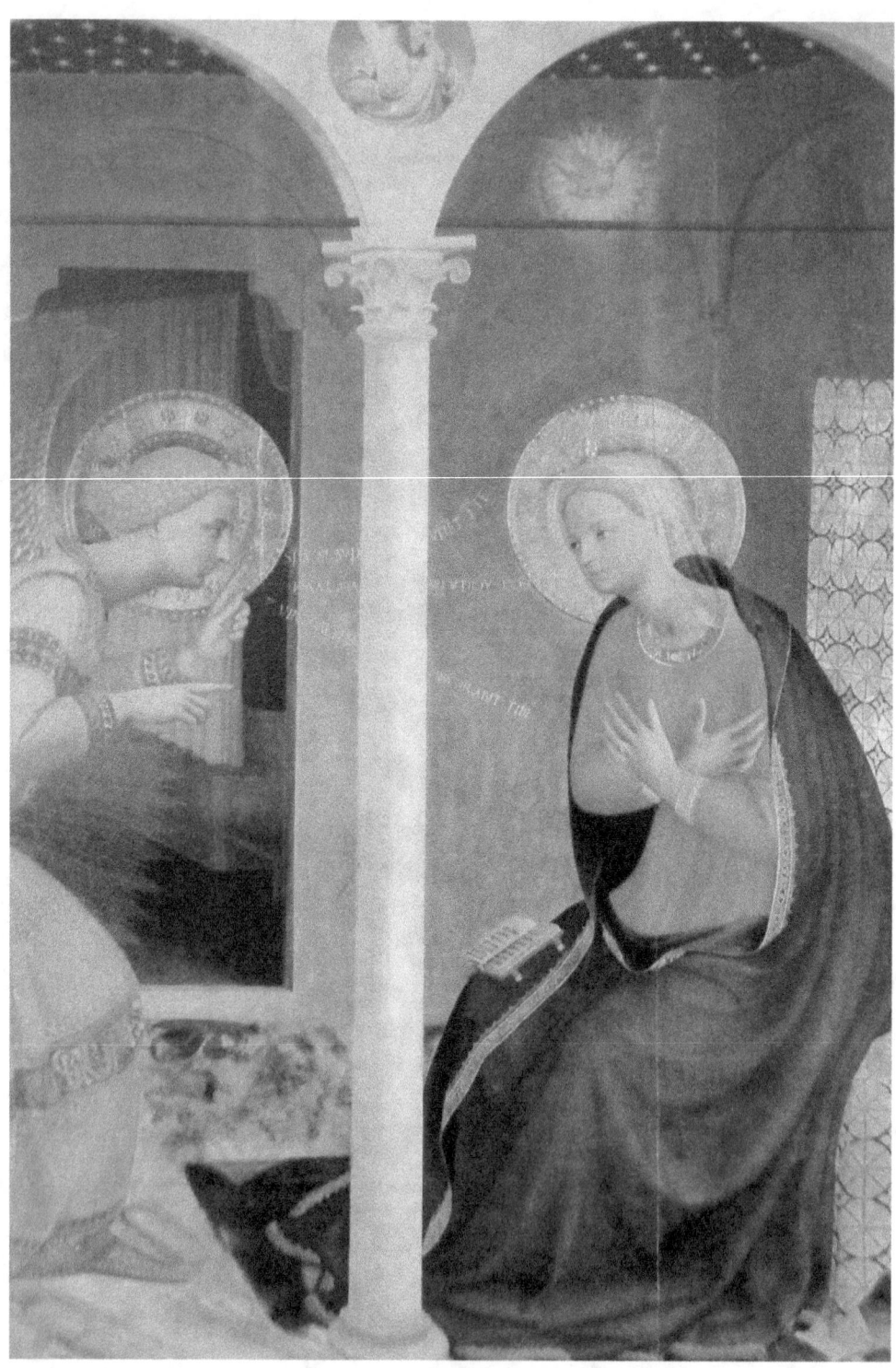

Fra Angelico, Anunciation, Cortona

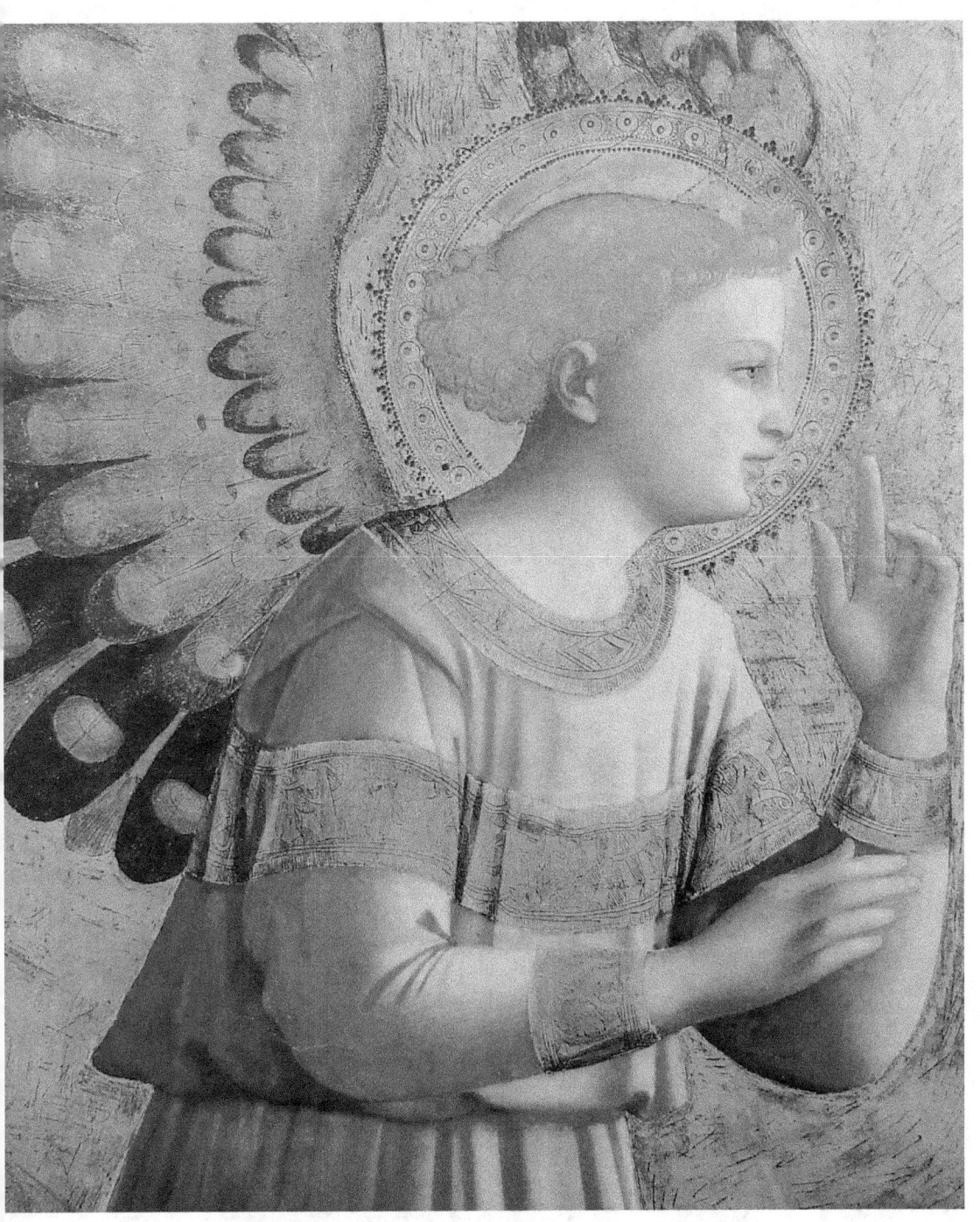

Fra Angelico, Annunciatory Angel, c. 1437-46, Detroit Institute of Arts

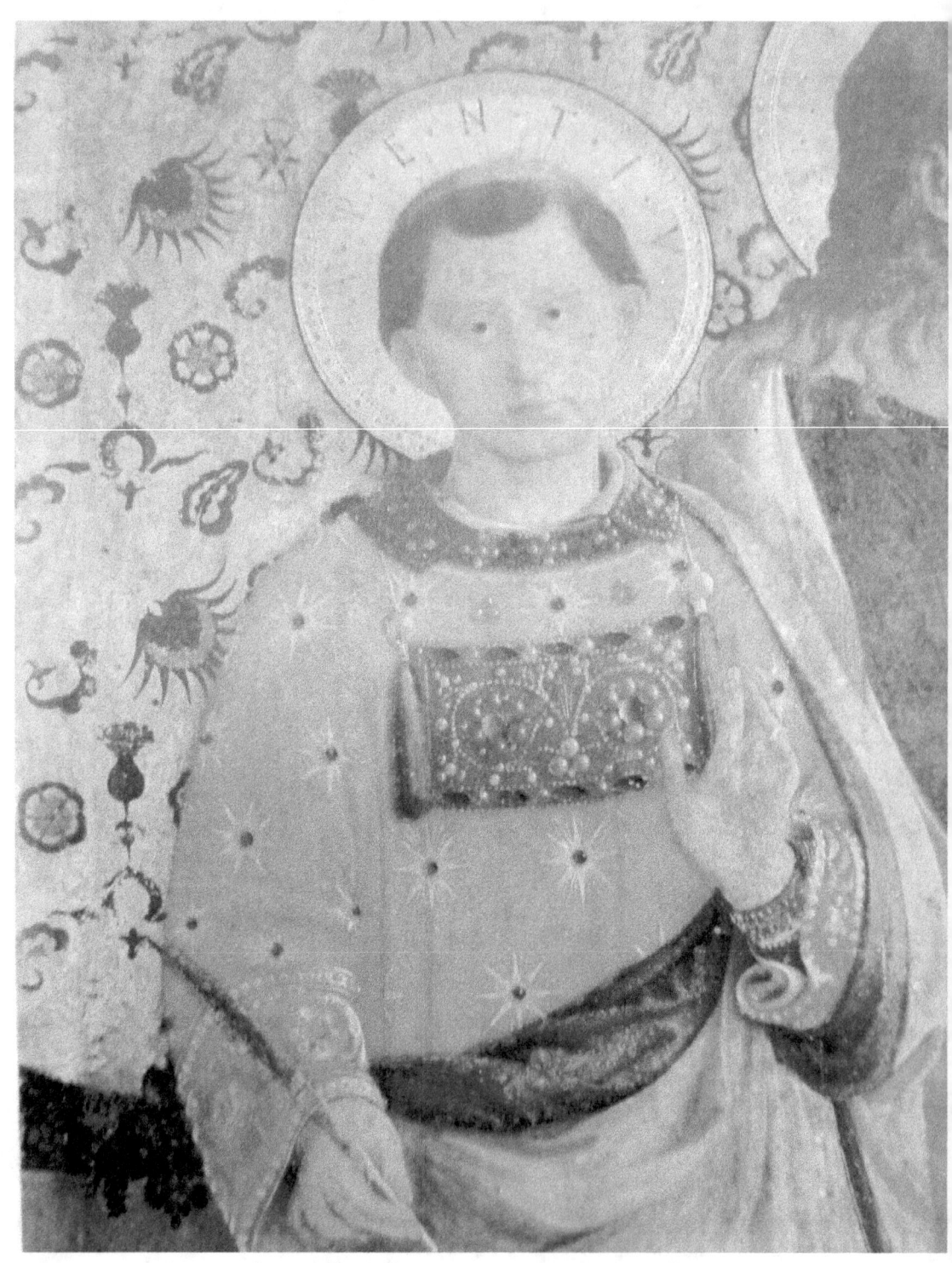

Fra Angelico, San Marco Altarpiece, 1438-40, detail

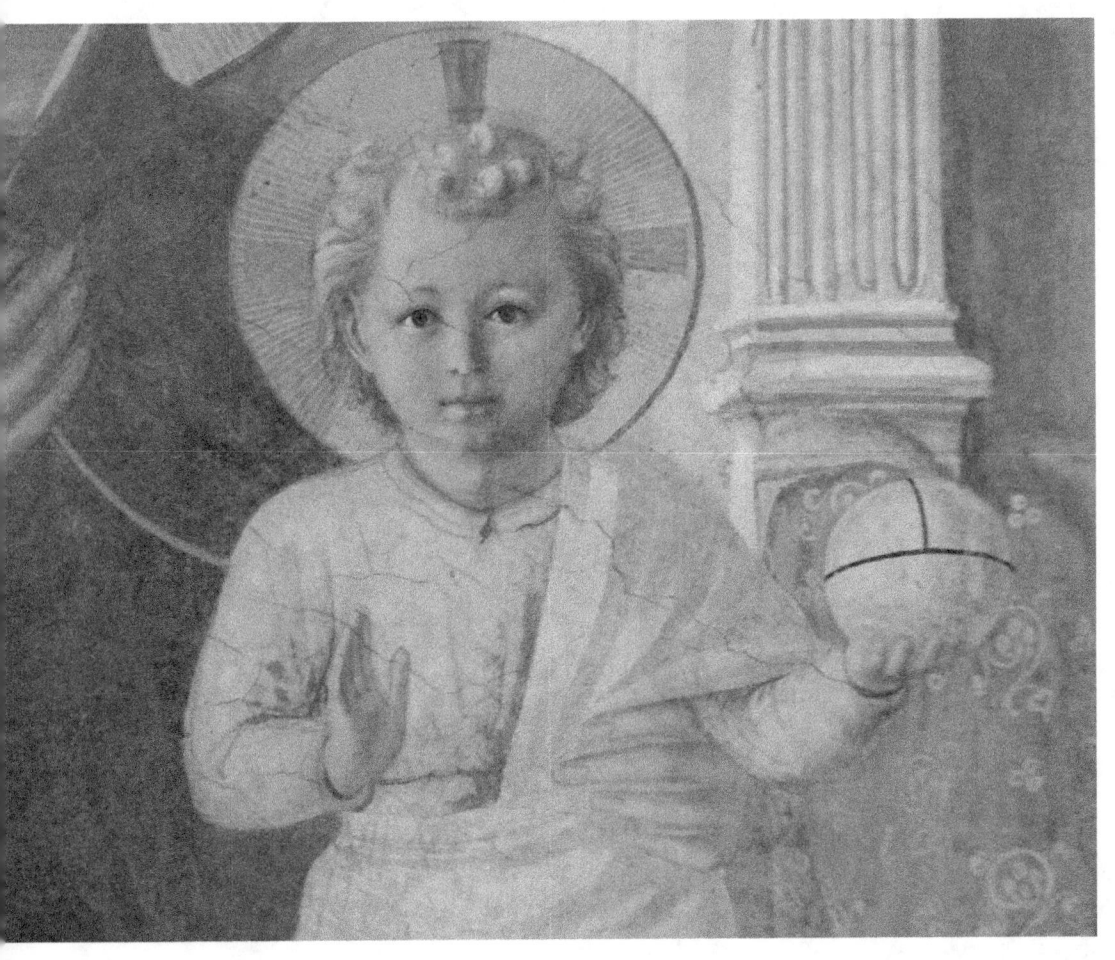

Fra Angelico, Virgin and Child Enthroned, c. 1450, detail, San Marco

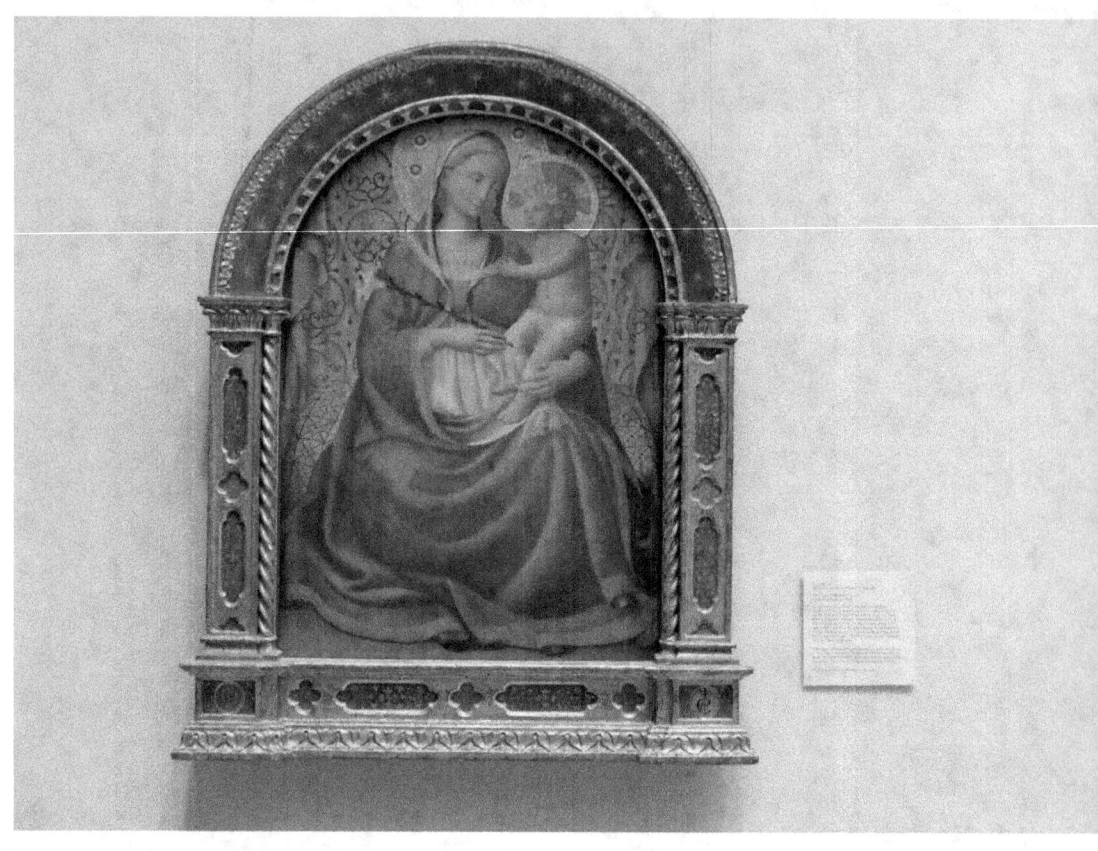

Fra Angelico, Madonna and Child, Metropolitan Museum of Art, New York

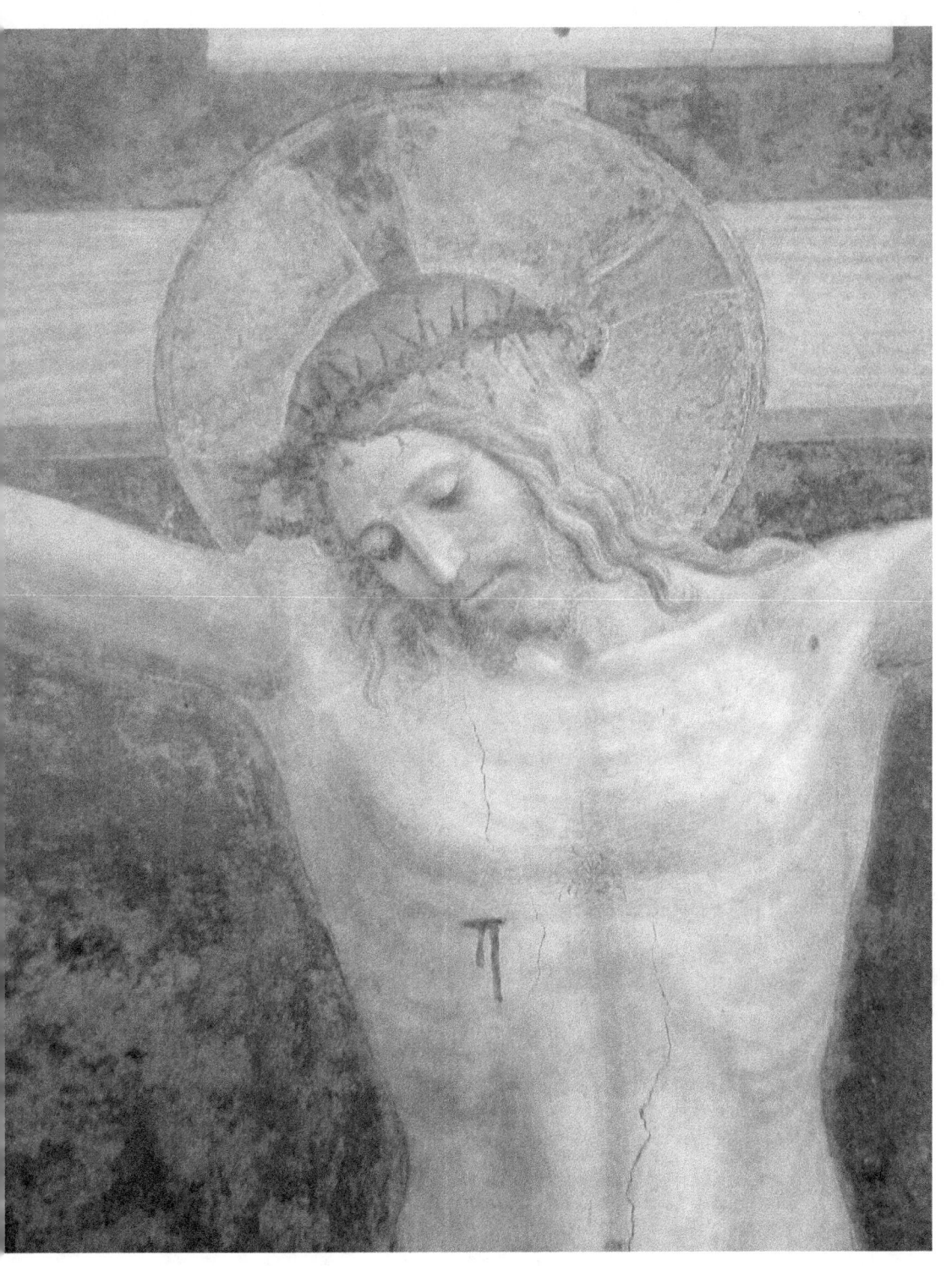

Fra Angelico, Christ On the Cross, c. 1442, detail, San Marco

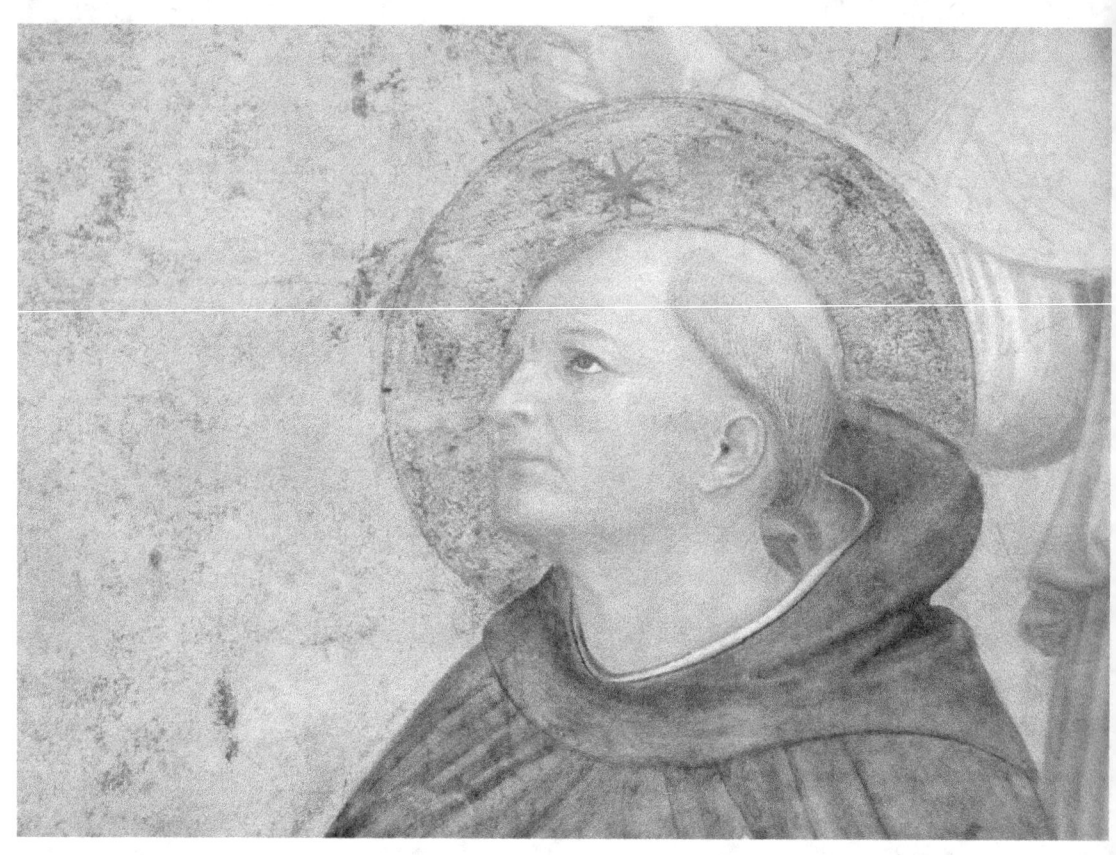

Fra Angelico, Crucifixion, detail, 1441-42, San Marco

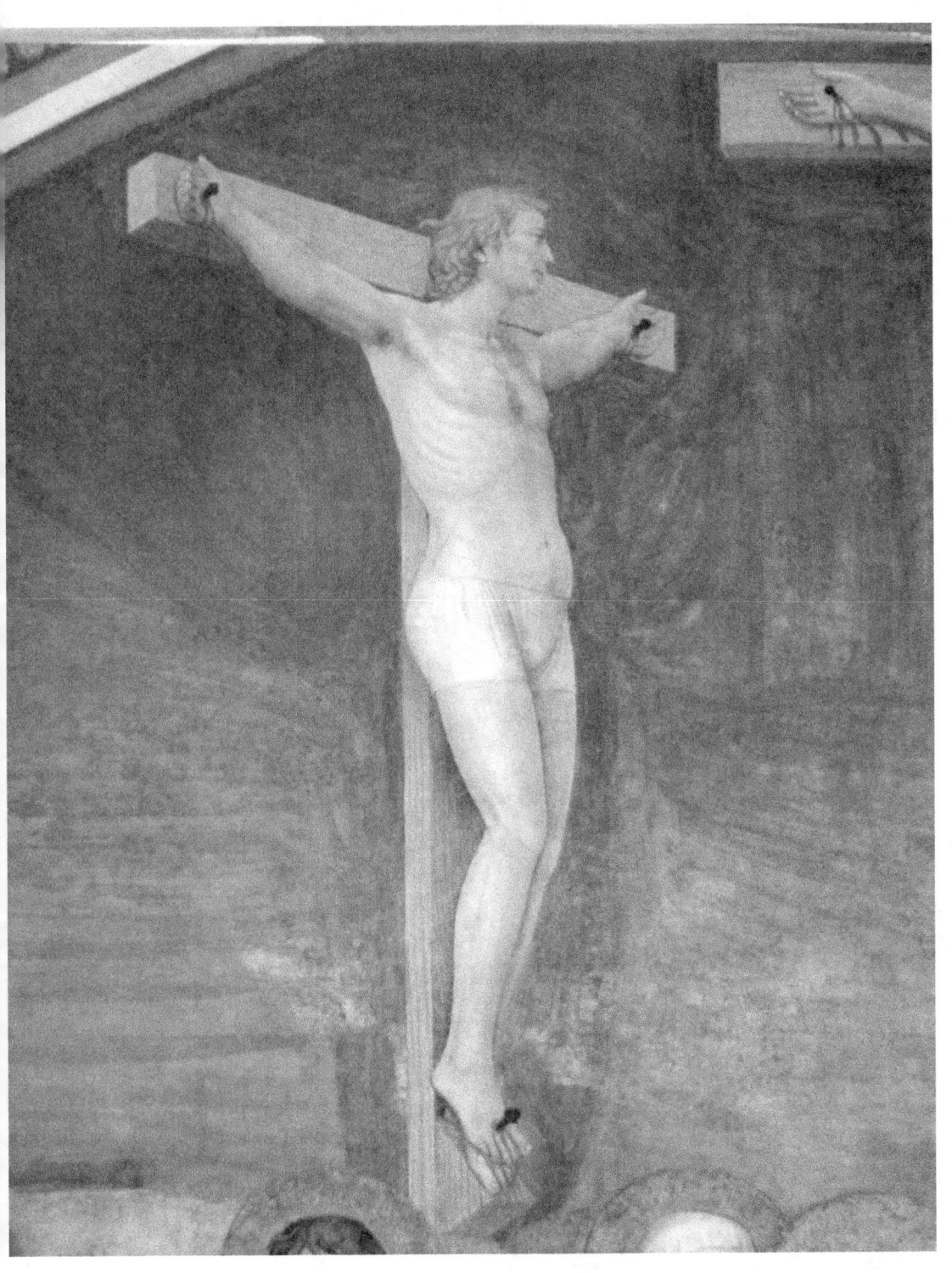

Fra Angelico, Crucifixion, 1441-42, San Marco, detail

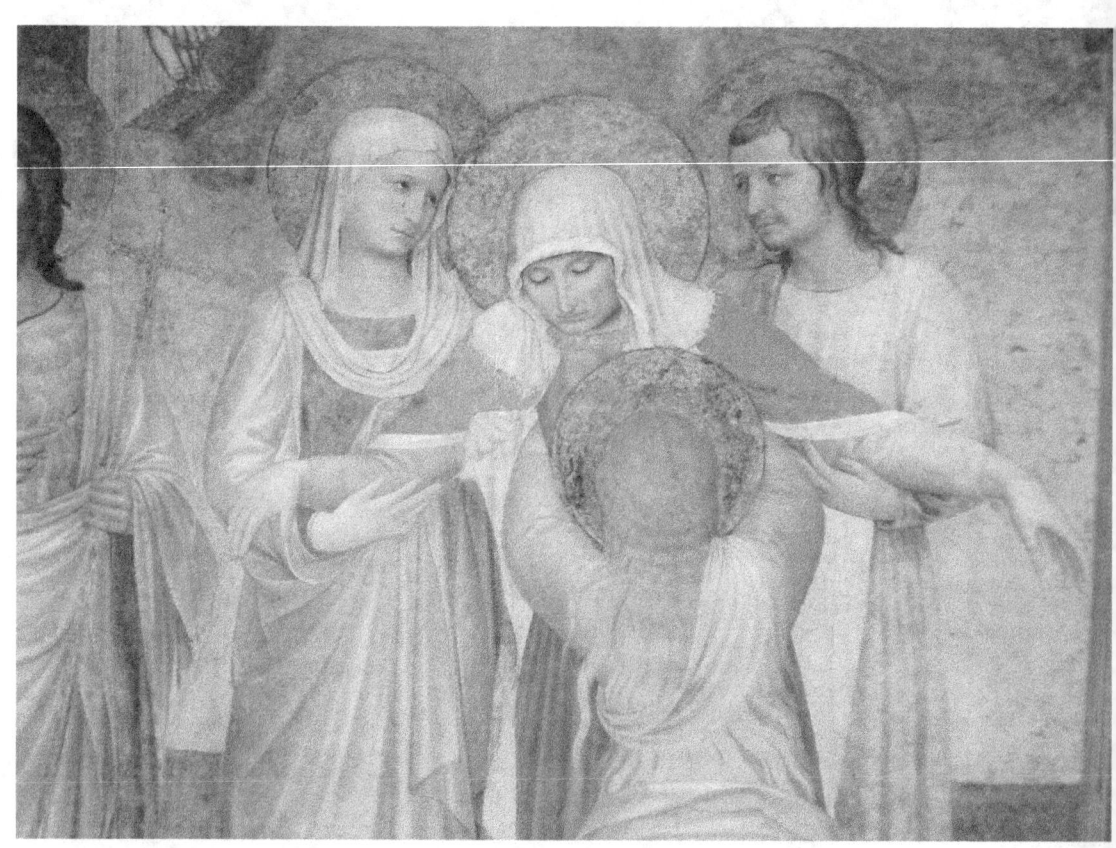

Fra Angelico, Crucifixion, detail

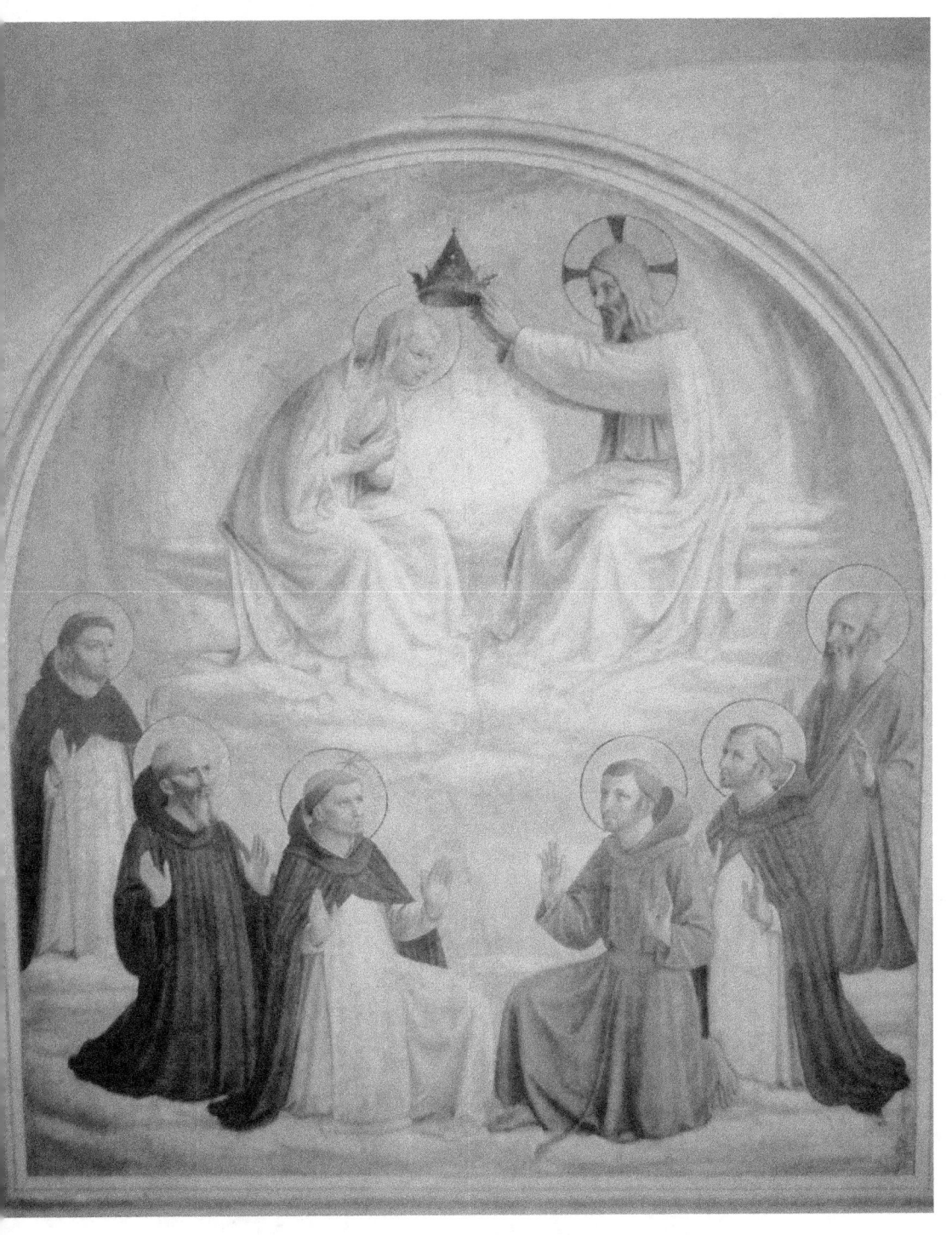

Fra Angelico, The Coronation of the Virgin, San Marco

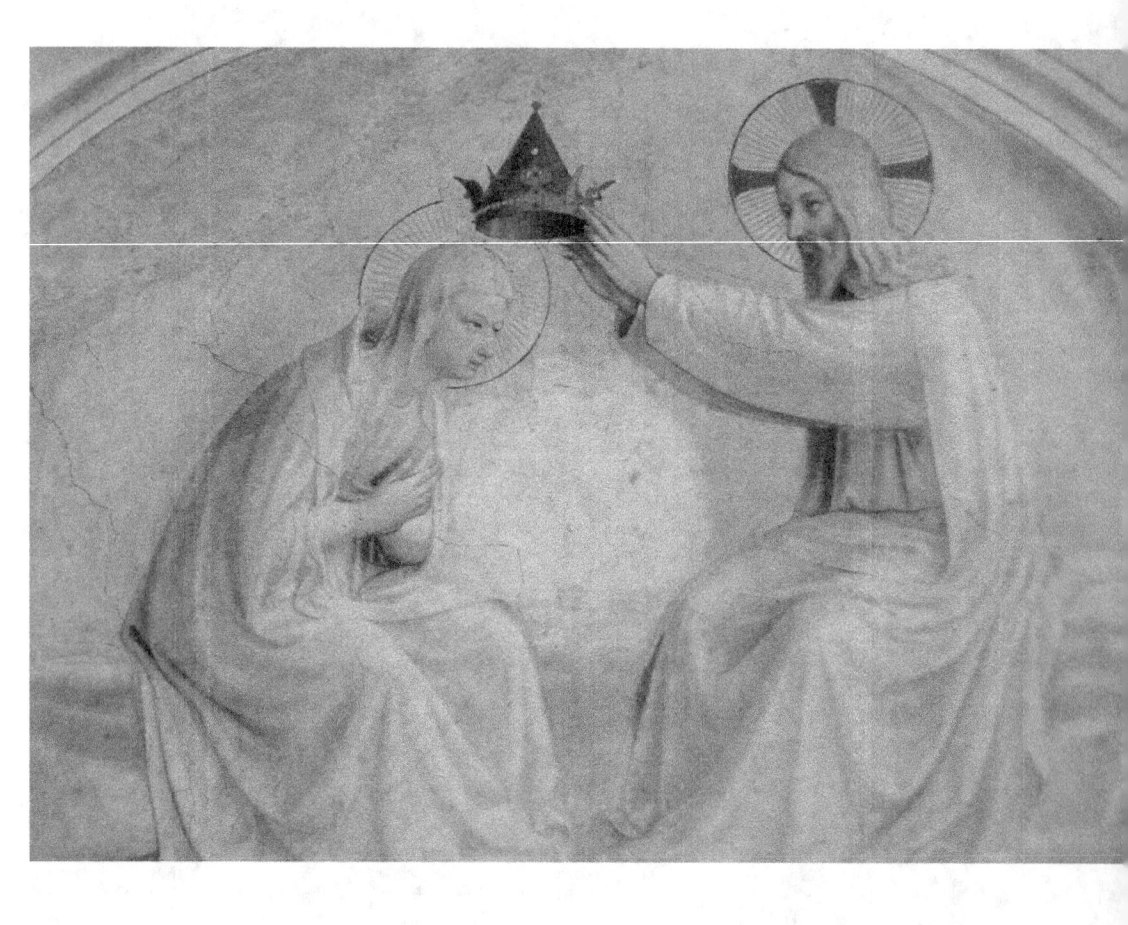

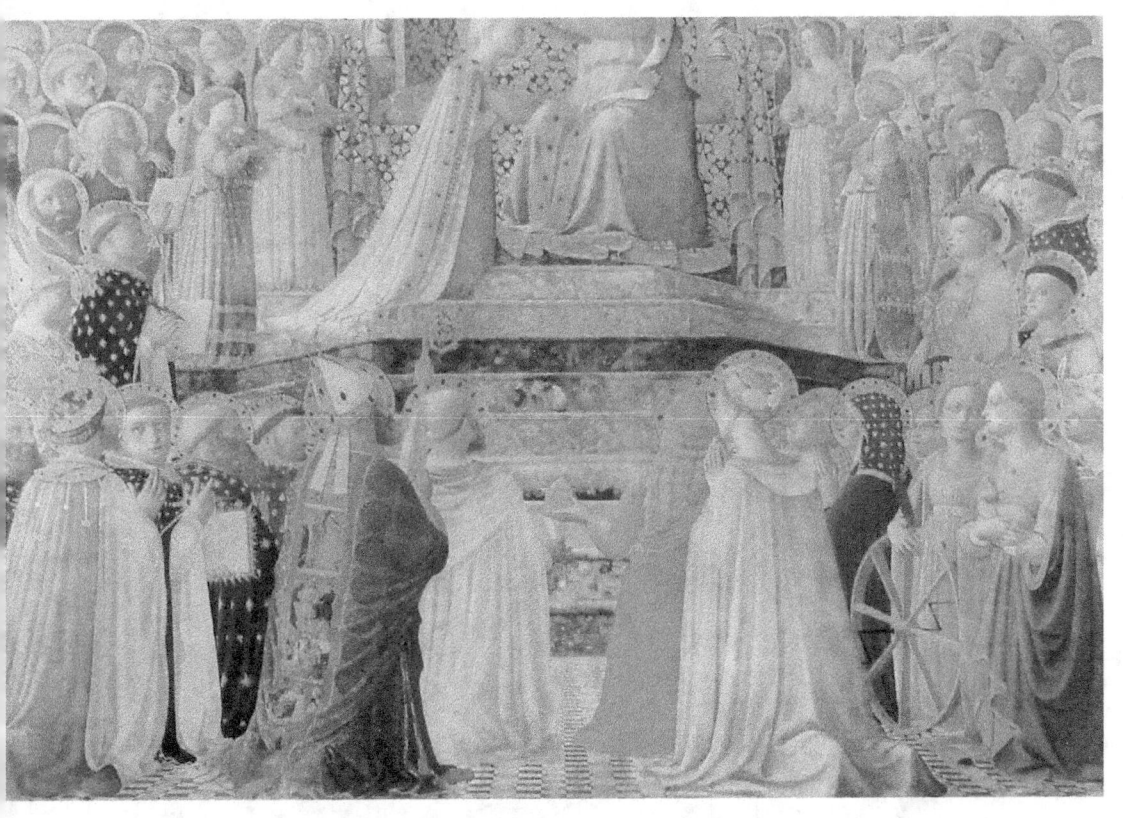

Fra Angelico, The Coronation of the Virgin, Louve, Paris, detail

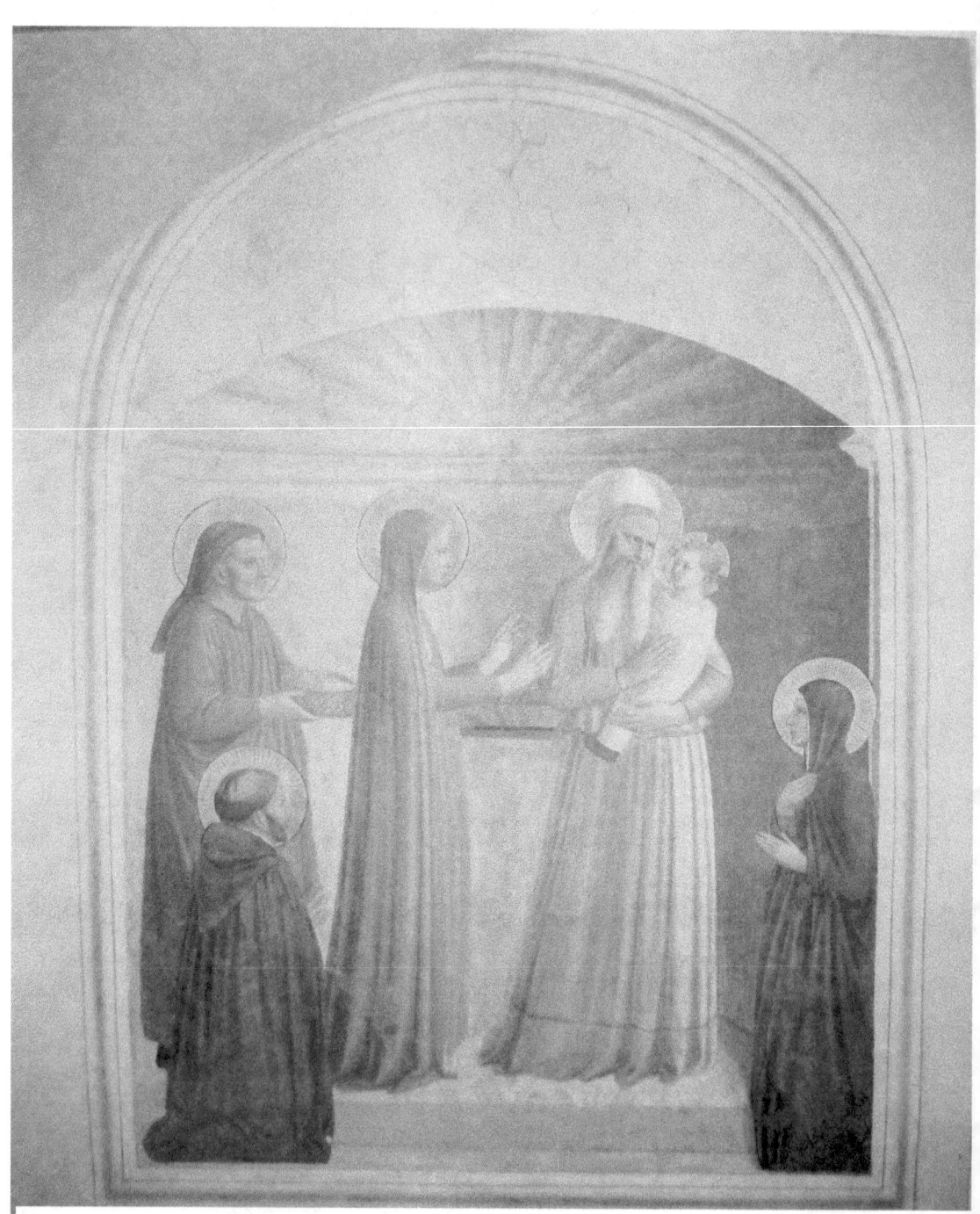

Fra Angelico, Presentation In the Temple, San Marco

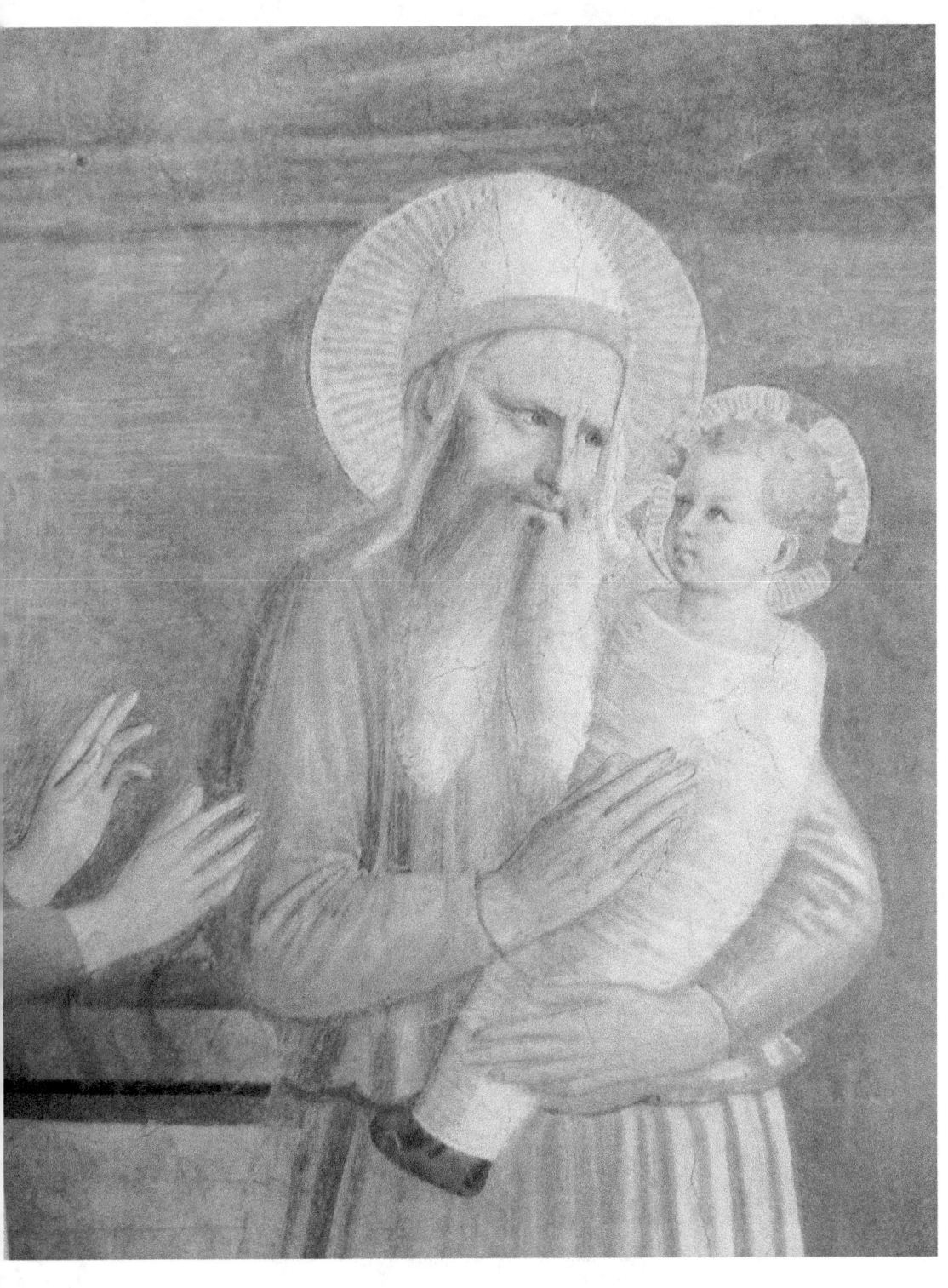

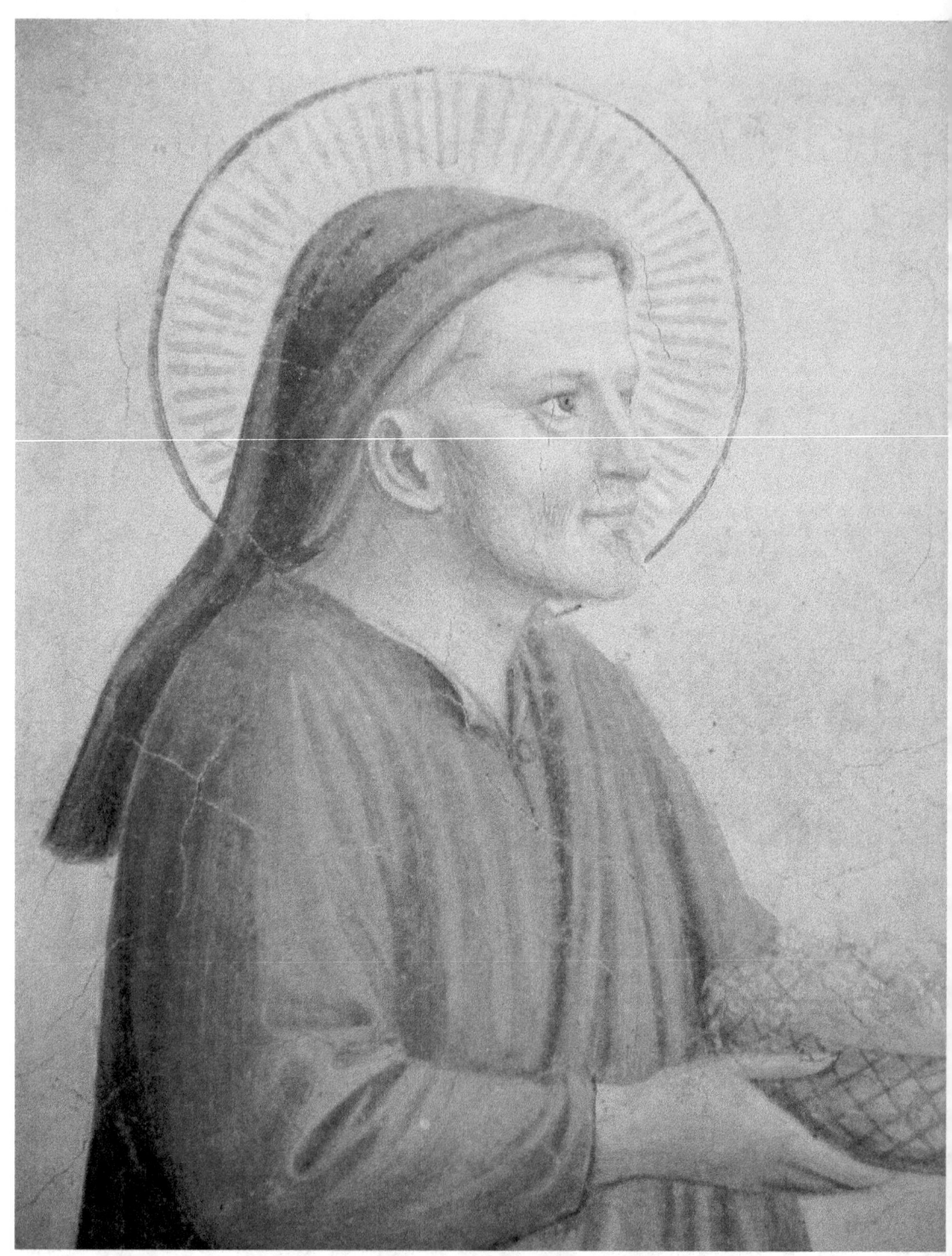

Fra Angelico, Presentation In the Temple, 1440-41, San Marco

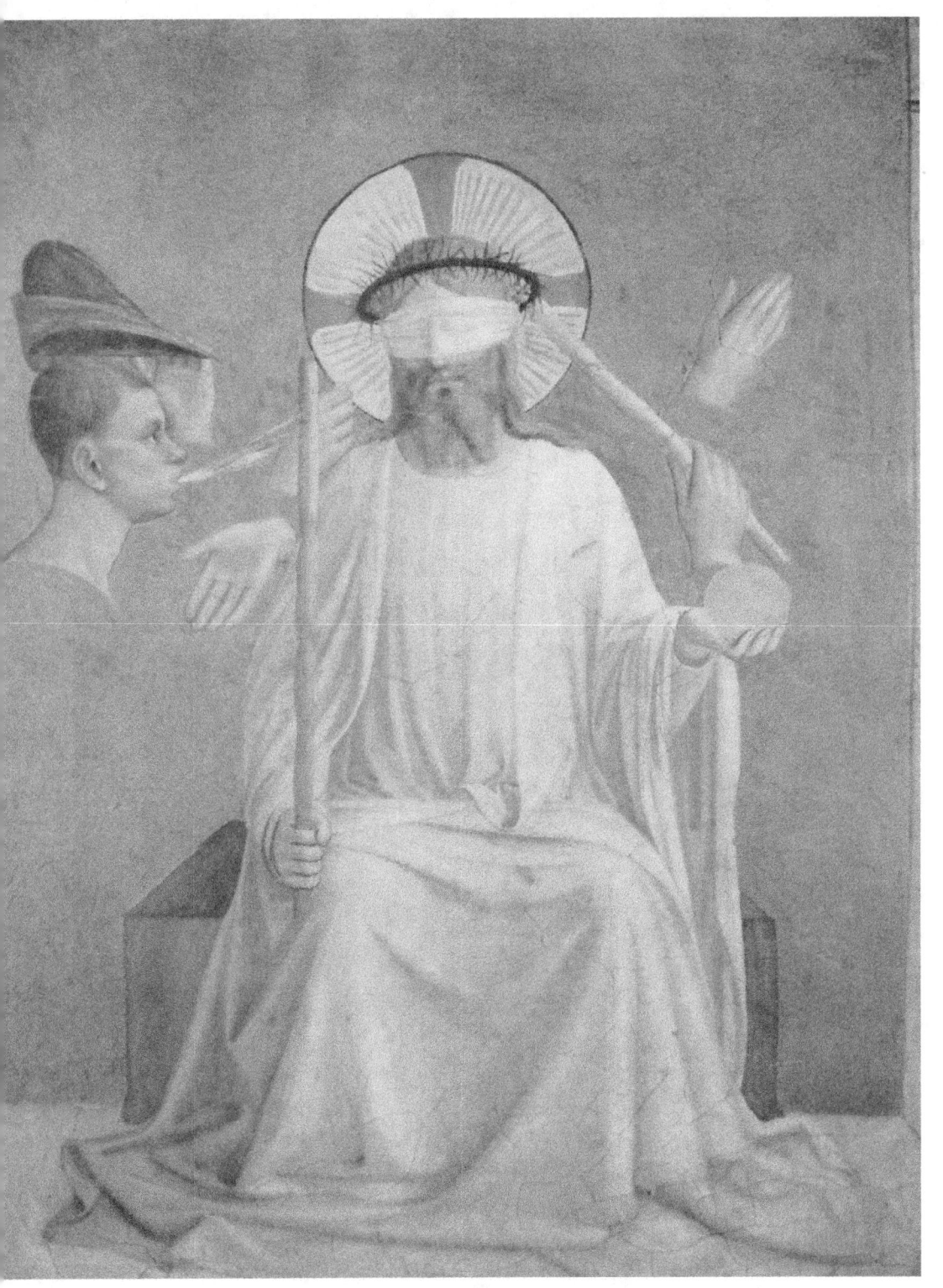

Fra Angelico, The Mocking of Christ, San Marco

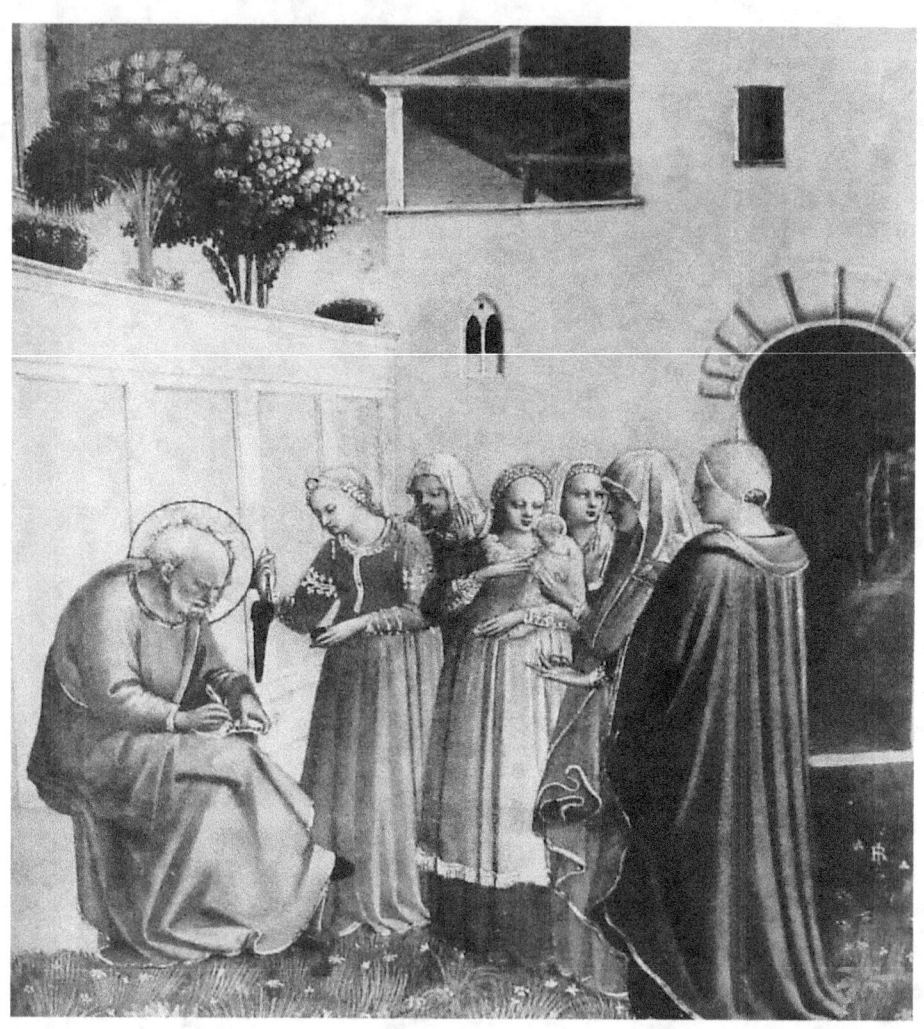

Fra Angelico, The Naming of John the Baptist, 1435

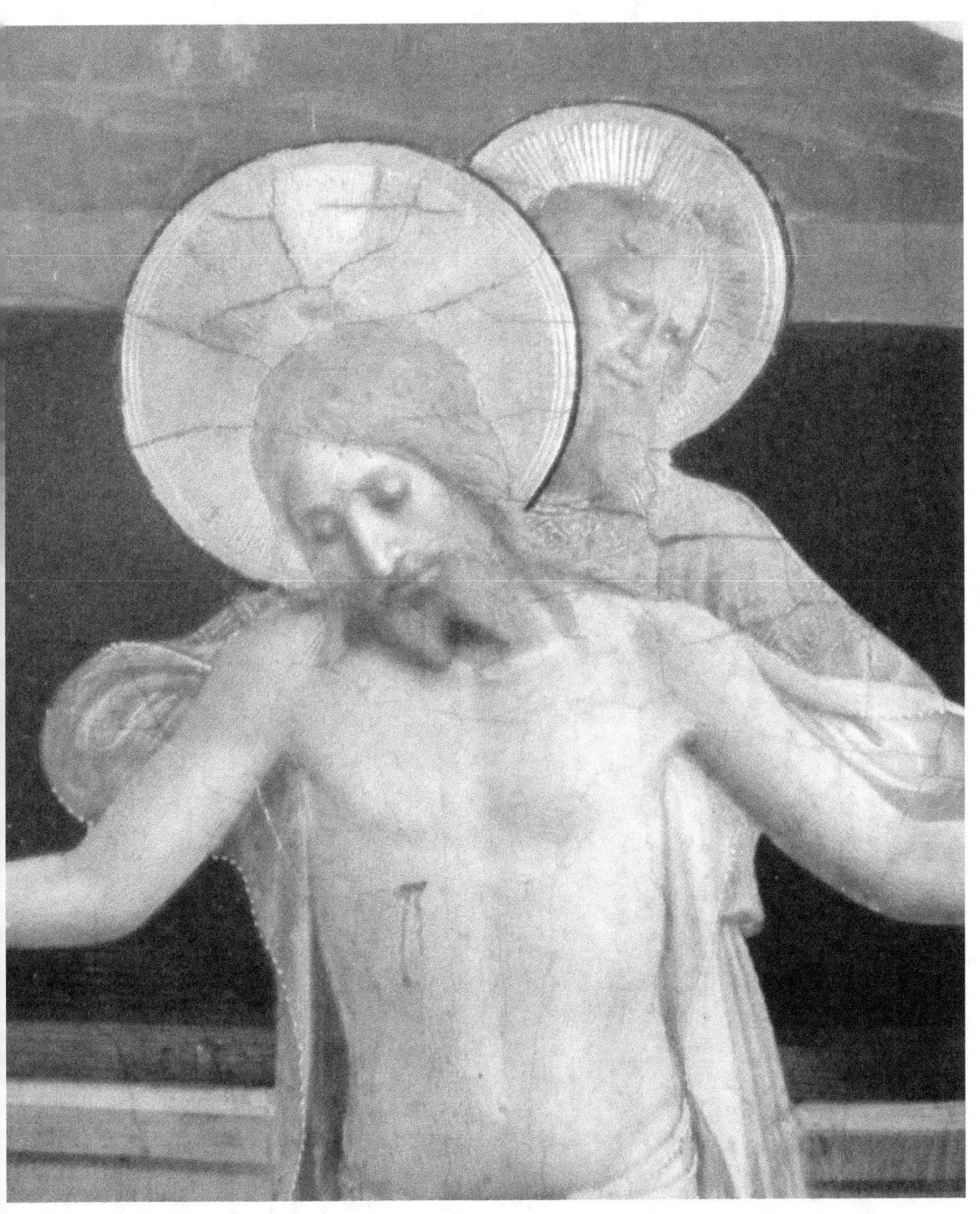

Fra Angelico, Lamentation Over the Dead Christ,
Alte Pinakothek, Munich, detail

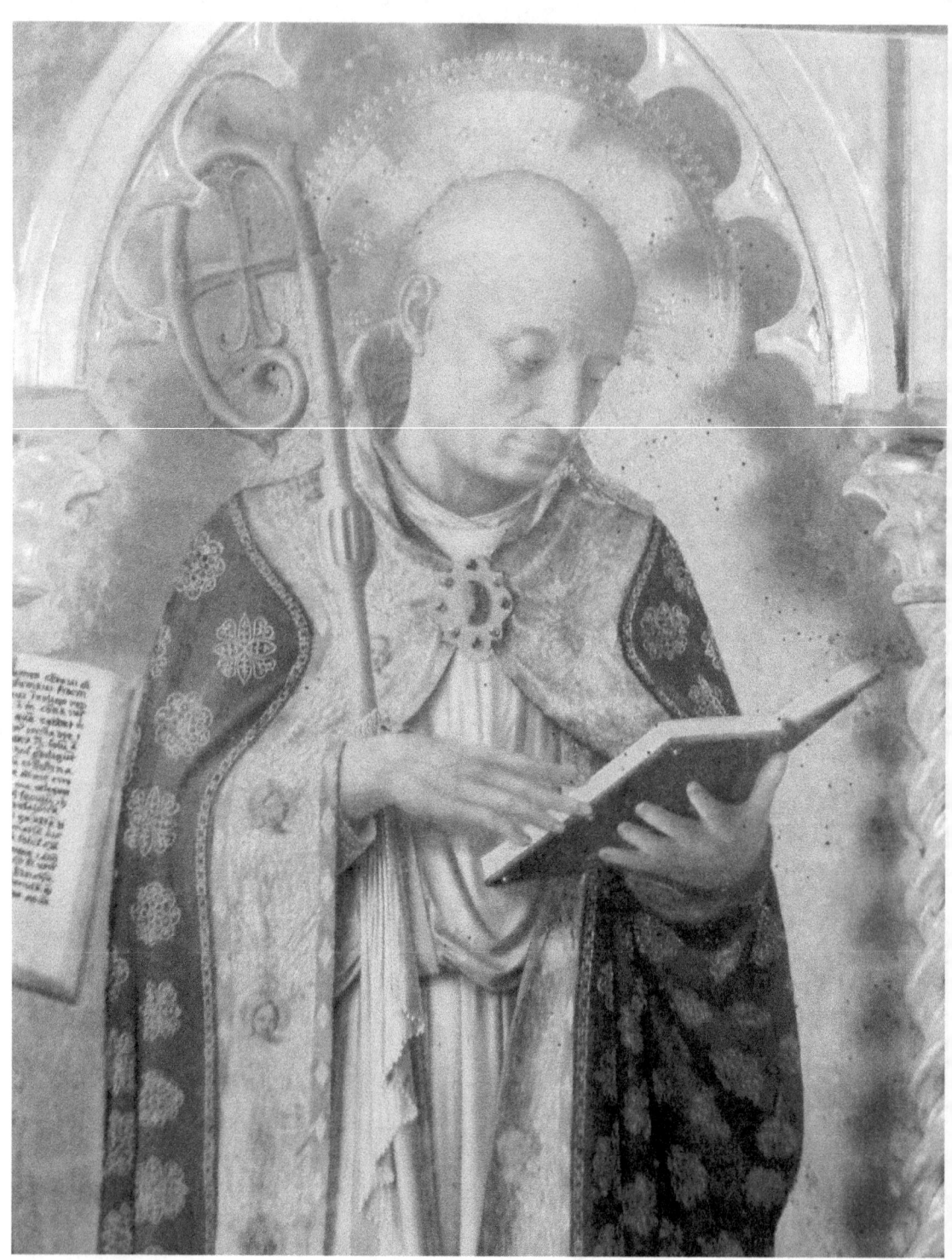

Fra Angelico, Perugia Altarpiece, 1448, detail

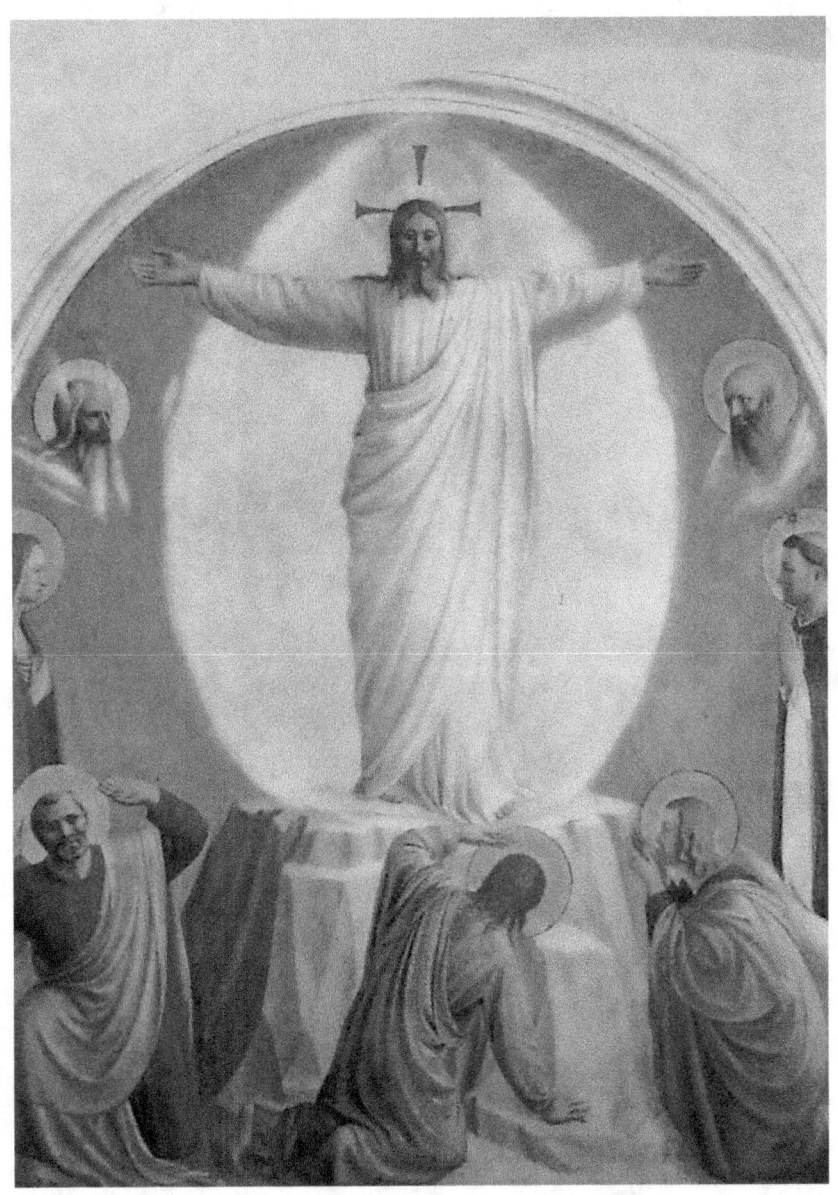

Fra Angelico, The Resurrection, San Marco, Florence

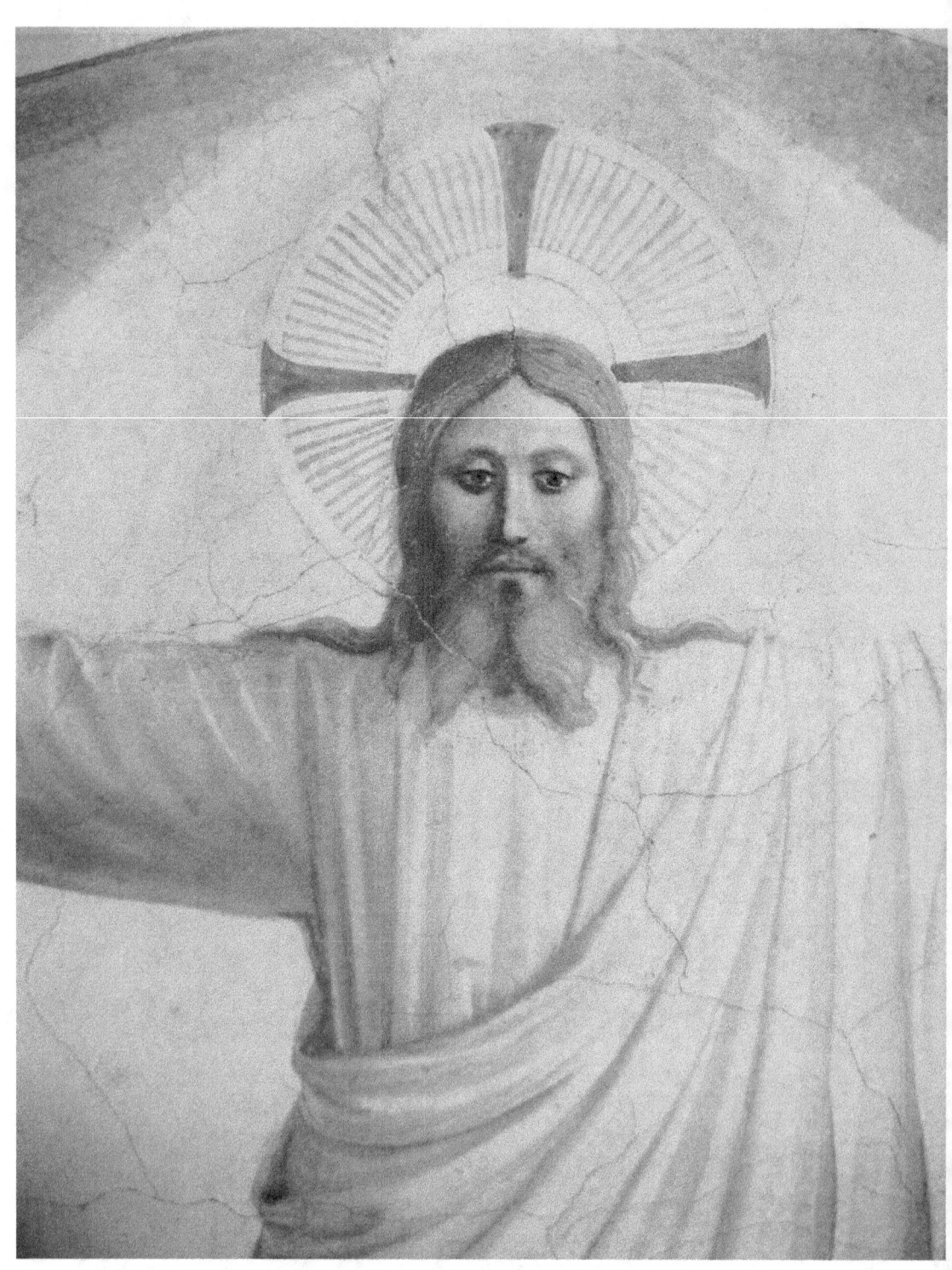

Fra Angelico, The Transfiguration, 1440-41, San Marco, detail

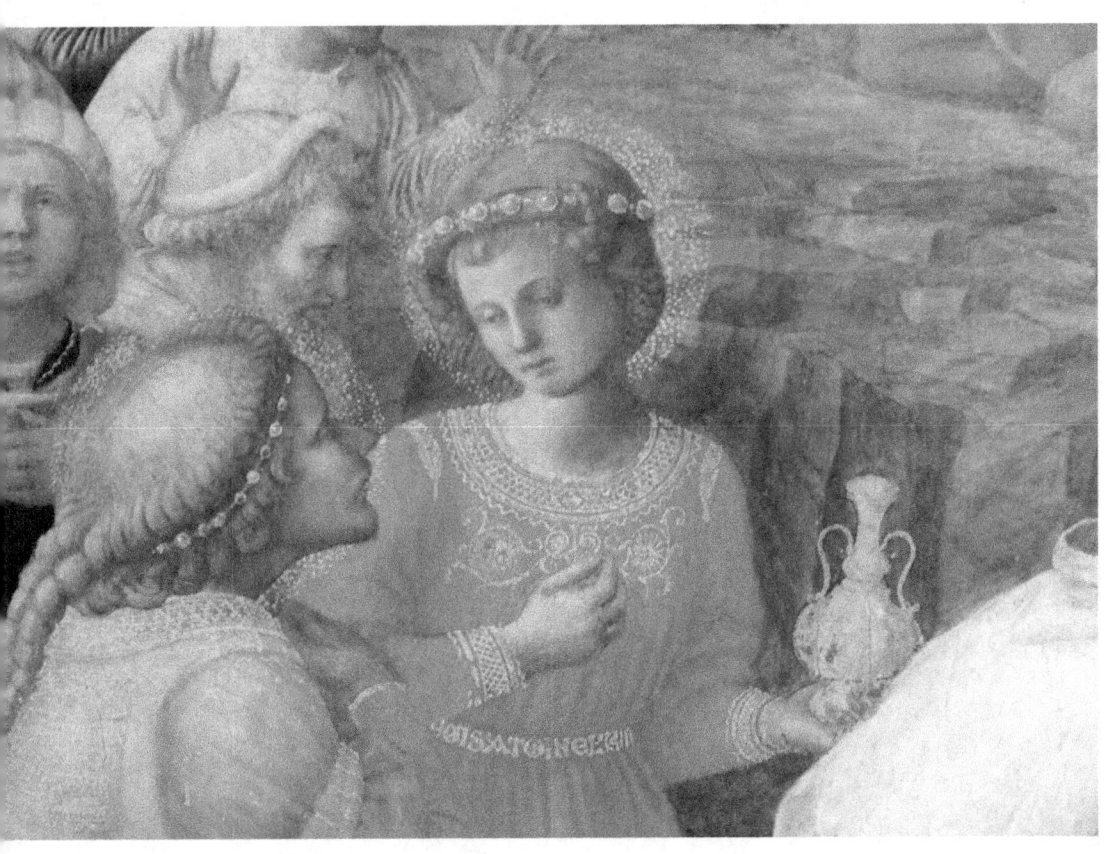

Fra Angelico, detail of Adoration of the Magi, 1445,
National Gallery of Art, Washington, DC (photo: author)

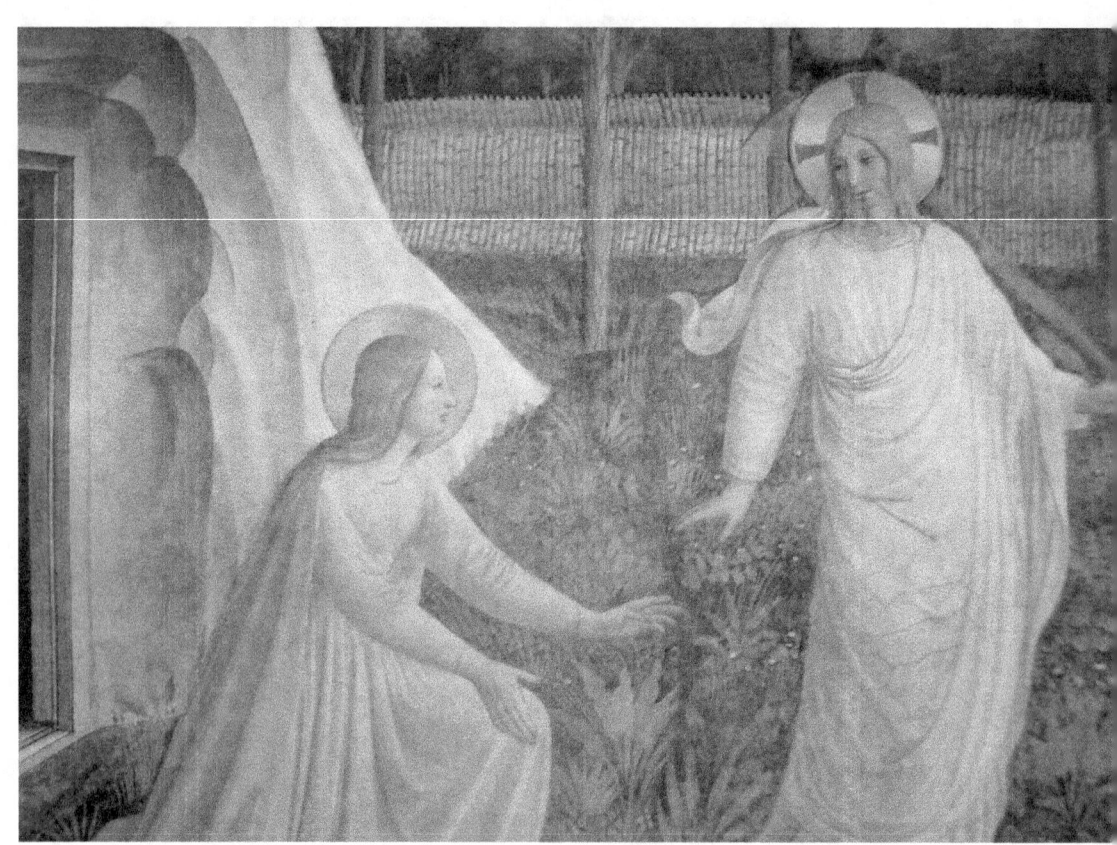

Fra Angelico, Noli Me Tangere

III

IN SAN MARCO

It was in 1435, and Fra Angelico was approaching his fiftieth year, when the brotherhood of San Dominico quitted their convent in Fiesole and went to find a new home in Florence. With the turn of the year they left a temporary resting-place in San Giorgio Oltr' Arno and went into the ruined monastery of San Marco. This house appears to have belonged to the brotherhood of San Silvestro whose behaviour had been quite fitted to the fifteenth century in Florence, but was not altogether creditable to a religious house. Pope Eugenius IV., anxious to purify all the religious houses, gave San Marco to the Dominicans with the consent of Cosimo di Medici, and a very poor gift it was at the time, for the dormitory had been destroyed by fire, and hastily-made wooden cabins could not keep out the rain and cold wind. There was a great mortality among the brethren. Once again the Pope Eugenius interceded with the powerful ruler of Florence, and Cosimo sent for his well-beloved architect Michelozzo and commissioned him to rebuild the monastery. Naturally enough Fra Angelico, whose feeling for architecture was finely developed, came under the influence of the architect, and when the building was complete he was commissioned to adorn the walls with frescoes that should keep before the brethren the actualities of the religious life, and enable them to feel that the Spiritual Presence was in their midst.

Cosimo's munificence had not stopped with the presentation of the building to the brotherhood. He equipped the monastery with a famous library, provided all the service books that were necessary, and gave the brethren for librarian a man who was destined to ascend the Fisherman's Throne and keep the keys of Heaven. The books were illuminated by Fra Angelico's brother Benedetto, who had taken the vows with him, indeed some critics are of opinion that Fra Angelico himself assisted in the work, but for this belief there appears to be but a very small foundation.

The Pope Eugenius, compelled by the quarrels of the great houses in Rome to leave the Eternal City, came to Florence and saw Fra Angelico's work there, and this visit paved the way for the painter's sojourn in Rome in the last years of his life. Like so many of his contemporaries, Eugenius could find time amid theTo realise the life that the painter saw around him in the days when the Dominican brotherhood first went to San Marco, it is necessary to turn to some historian of Florence in an endeavour to recall the splendour and stateliness of the city's life. The limits of space forbid any attempt, however modest, to picture Florence in detail as it was in those days, though the subject could scarcely be more tempting to the pen. The pomp and circumstance of life were not passed over by the painter, whose extraordinary receptivity found so much more in Florence than in Fiesole for its exercise. Some echo, however, subdued to convent walls, lingers in the city to-day where San Marco preserves its great painter's reputation, and tells us that he was not indifferent to the sights and sounds beyond its gates.

A few of the frescoes have lost a little of their pristine beauty and yet, for all the ravages of time, the most faded among them can suggest much of the charm they possessed when they were painted. It is in the open cloisters, of course, that the greatest damage has been done, and the great "Crucifixion" in the chapter-house has not escaped lightly; but in the cells where the work is more protected, time has dealt lightly with the frescoes and the two or three little panels that help to make the friar's lasting monument. Good judges have pointed out that the great "Crucifixion" in the chapter-house, the largest work of the painter, was never completed, and that the red background was intended to serve as a bed for the blue that was never put on. Nobody can say why this fine work was abandoned, and reproduction in colour is impossible. Even a detail would be unsatisfactory, but one of the lunettes from the cloister is given here. It represents Christ as a pilgrim meeting two Dominican brothers, and gives an excellent suggestion of Fra Angelico at his best, revealing the deep feeling of the religious man, and the skill of the artist blended together in happiest and most inspired union. To have seen the picture in his mind, the artist must have been a deeply religious man; to have expressed the vision as he has expressed it in terms of line and colour, the devotee must have been a great artist.

From one of the cells in San Marco the chief part of another picture has been reproduced in these pages. It represents the "Coronation of the Virgin." Christ seated upon a white cloud is placing a crown upon the Virgin's head; there is a rainbow border with six saints. In order that the beauty of the central figures may be seen, no more than a part of the picture is given here. It is the more important part, for the saints are conventional figures, each with the hands uplifted in adoration, each with a halo round his head. The beauty of the stories that Fra Angelico sets before us was as true to him as the beauty of the flowers he painted, and the landscape that met his eyes whenever he walked abroad. The modern world, whether it doubt or believe, cannot but recognise that the artist of San Marco has succeeded as much by his faith as by his art. The other frescoes of the Dominican House must be left for the fortunate minority who can visit them, but these two will be found to represent well and truthfully both the religious idea and the artistic achievement. To realise their merits to the full one must not fail to bear in mind the development of painting at the time when they were painted. For the men who came after Angelico the task was easier; he had paved the way for them. In the days when San Marco was decorated, the painter had very little to add to his technical knowledge, and nothing at all to his feeling for the beauty of the Gospel stories, and few artists of the fifteenth century have been so fortunate as to collect their best work in one place where it could remain undisturbed throughout the ages.

Naturally enough it must pass – cloisters and chapter-house show signs of the times all too clearly. "The Crucifixion" is faded not so badly as Leonardo's "Last Supper" in the Santa Maria della Grazie of Milan, but still seriously, nor can all the *lire* of faithful but hurried tourists restore its charm. It is in the cells that the work of Fra Angelico will linger longest, and it is pleasant to speculate upon the debt that devout monks must have owed to their artist brother, who could give them such exquisite embodiments of the truth as he saw it to brighten their hard lives and assure them, even in hours of doubt and mental trouble, of the joys that would be associated with the latter end.

San Marco, then, may be regarded as an exquisite and enduring memorial of the middle period of Fra Angelico's life. The saint that was in him dreamed dreams and saw visions, the artist that was in him expressed them in fashion that calls for admiration even in these days when the work done is nearly four hundred years old, and the thought that gave it birth is no longer held in such universal esteem. The devotion that inspired the themes, the simplicity of his handling, the beauty of his colour, the love of Nature that was expressed as often as the picture would permit, the reverential feeling in treatment that was bound to communicate itself to the spectator, all these qualities make the work remarkable, and help us to see how strong was the faith that inspired and kept the artist happy in the cloisters when, had he wished to turn his talent to other purposes, he might have had riches and honour. Leading rulers of men were building palaces in every great city, conquerors and statesmen were seeking to excel one another in tasteful and costly display. Of those who could have commanded wealth, honour, and comfort, the Dominican friar was among the first. But it sufficed Fra Angelico to serve neither kings nor princes, but to choose for his worship the King of kings "Who made the heavens and the earth and all that is therein."

IV

LATER YEARS

There is a great temptation to linger awhile in San Marco with the friar, for even to-day the place has not lost its appeal, and there are sufficient landmarks in the surrounding city to enable us to trace the influence of men who were at once the contemporaries and inspirers of his genius. Only the limits of space intervene to forbid too long a stay in Florence, and as the painter's later years were spent in Rome we must follow him there. For those who wish to linger in the monastery there are books in plenty, some dealing with the Quattrocento, others dealing with the Popes, others with Fra Angelico himself. This outline of a painter's life seeks to do no more than introduce him to those who may be interested; it is not intended for those who wish to follow him beyond the limits of a modest appreciation. Vasari, Crowe, and Cavalcaselle, Professor Langton Douglas, Bernhard Berenson and others will supply the more complete and detailed accounts of the painter's life and works, and the careful reader will find sufficient references to other writers to direct him to every side issue.

Pope Eugenius IV., who visited Florence when he was exiled from Rome, had settled for a while in Bologna until the anti-Pope Felix V. fell from power, and had then hastened back to Rome, and settled down to beautify the Vatican. Like all the great men of his generation he felt the spirit of the Renaissance in the air, and desired no more than leisure in order to respond to it. He remembered the clever artist, whose work had charmed him in the days of his Florentine exile, and sent an invitation to Fra Angelico to come to Rome and decorate one of the chapels in the Vatican. In those days one travelled in Italy, even more slowly than one does to-day by the Italian express trains – strange as the statement may seem to moderns who know the country well – and by the time that the friar had received the summons and had responded to it, Eugenius IV. would appear to have relinquished the keys to his successor. Happily the new Pope Nicholas V. was a scholar, a gentleman, and a statesman, as responsive to the new ideas as his predecessor in office. He gathered the best men of his time to the Vatican, which he proposed to rebuild, and he entered upon a programme that could scarcely have been carried out had he enjoyed a much longer lease of life than Providence granted. Unfortunately he had no more than eight years to rule at St. Peter's, and that did not serve for much more than a beginning of his great scheme. He was succeeded by Tomaso Parentucelli, that ardent scholar whom Cosimo di Medici had appointed custodian of the collection of MSS. that he gave to San Marco in Florence when the Dominicans took possession. As it happened Parentucelli himself was in the last year of his life when he ascended the throne of St. Peter, and his schemes, whether for the aid and development of scholarship or art, saw no fruition. But for all that Nicholas V. ruled for no more than eight years in Rome, he did much for Fra Angelico, who painted the frescoes in the Pope's private studio, and decorated a chapel in St. Peter's that was afterwards destroyed. This loss is of course a very serious one, and suggests that those who ruled in the Vatican were not always as careful as they might have been of works that would have outlived them so long had they been fairly treated. It is very unfortunate that art should suffer from the caprices of the unintelligent. When Savonarola, also a Dominican monk, roused the Florentines to a sense of their lapses from grace a few years after Fra Angelico's death, they made a bonfire in the streets of Florence of art work that was considered immoral. To sacrifice great work in the name of morality is bad enough, to destroy it for the sake of building operations is quite unpardonable.

In Rome the summer heat is well-nigh unbearable. Even to-day the voluntary prisoner of the Vatican retires to a villa in the far end of his gardens towards the end of June, and none who can leave the city cares to remain in it when May has gone, and the Tiber becomes a thread, and fever haunts its banks. Fra Angelico felt the burden of the summer and wished to suspend his work for a while. It so happened that he received an invitation from Orvieto to decorate the Duomo there during the months of June, July, and August. The first arrangement was that he should go there every summer to escape the dog-days in Rome, but for reasons not known to us the visit did not extend beyond one year, and the frescoes that he had painted were seriously injured by rain, and were not completed until Luca Signorelli took them in hand half a century later. The little work that is attributed to the painter's brush to-day in Orvieto need not detain us here.

The frescoes in Rome represent the summit of Fra Angelico's achievement, but they have not escaped the somewhat destructive hand of nineteenth-century German criticism; one eminent authority having declared that they are not by Fra Angelico at all, but have been painted by pupils, Benozzo Gozzoli receiving special mention in this connection. It is not necessary to take this criticism too seriously. The hands may be the hands of Esau, but "the voice is Jacob's voice." The artist may have received some assistance from pupils, the backgrounds may owe something to another hand; there was no feeling, ethical or artistic, to keep assistants from coming to the aid of their master, but the whole composition and the whole feeling of the frescoes proclaim the friar. The subjects are incidents in the life of St. Stephen and St. Lorenzo, ending, of course, after the inevitable fashion of the time, with a representation of the martyrdom. For once these martyrdoms have a suggestion of reality. In the early days of Fra Angelico's work his representations of martyrdoms and suffering were so naïve that they could hardly do more than provoke a smile. His idea of hell was very simple, and when he wished to be very bitter indeed – to express his anger at its fullest – he peopled the nether world with brothers of the great rival order of St. Francis. For the founder of that order, Angelico had the greatest love and admiration; who indeed could refuse to pay such tribute even to-day? But all the brethren did not live up to the rule of their founder, and the Dominican painter's rebuke seems very quaint in our eyes, though doubtless it made a great sensation when it was administered.

In Rome the painter's feeling for natural beauty reaches the height of its expression, indeed one feels that every department of his work is at its best and highest there. After his departure from the Eternal City, the frescoes finished, and himself on the shady side of his sixtieth year, the intervening centuries descend like a cloud, blotting out the greater part of the record. The cloud lifts for a moment to show us "Beato" Angelico, Prior of the Dominican Monastery at Fiesole, to which more than forty years ago he had claimed admission as a novice, and then he is back again in Rome in the chief convent of his order, Santa Maria Sopra Minerva. There the light that had burned so brilliantly for nearly half a century, illuminating the most alluring aspects of the Christian faith, paled and went out. The body was laid to rest in the convent Church, near the tomb of St. Catherine, and it is said that the epitaph was composed by the Pope. Thereafter the order of St. Dominic produced no great personality until it gave to the world a man of very different stamp in Fra Girolamo Savonarola.

V

A RETROSPECT

In art as in music and literature the path of the innovator is beset by difficulties, and if, among all the movements that claim our attention to-day, that of the Renaissance in fifteenth-century Italy is the most fascinating, it is because the difficulties were conquered so brilliantly. The century seemed to breed a race of men that enjoyed the inestimable advantage of knowing what they wanted, and were determined to succeed.

It did not matter that the paths they trod were new. Each man had mapped out a line of development for himself and went strenuously along his chosen road, quite certain that he would find the goal of his ambition at the journey's end. Curiously enough when the paths were those of conquest there was always a road leading from them to patronage of the arts. This may be because art in those days was largely devoted to the service of the Church, and when a man had acquired all that theft or conquest could give him, and realised that he could not hope to wage successful war upon time, he began to think of his latter days. Few men of the fourteenth and fifteenth centuries could approach death with confidence, and they sought to put something to their credit against the Day of Judgment. To beautify religious houses, to build houses for Holy Brotherhoods, these were the simplest and most obvious ways of placating the Recording Angel, and to the uneasiness of rich and unscrupulous men the Church owes not a few of her most remarkable monuments. Moreover, even the tyrants wished to have some enduring memorial. Cosimo di Medici, who gave San Lorenzo and San Marco to Florence, remarked to his historian Bisticci, "Fifty years will not pass before we are driven out of Florence, but these buildings will remain." After all we can forget and forgive the superstition and self-glorification that gave so much enduring wealth to the great cities of Italy.

Doubtless there were many failures among the Renaissance artists; it is hardly an exaggeration to say that in painting alone there are scores of men belonging to the Quattrocento who have left us nothing but their names. Victory was to the fittest; they alone survived and left the impress of their genius upon their own and succeeding generations. If we look for a moment to Fra Angelico's contemporaries we see at once that it was an age of great men. Filippo Brunelleschi was born ten years before Angelico, and lived until the year 1446. He designed the dome of the Cathedral of Florence, the Cloisters of San Lorenzo, the Sagrestia Vecchia, the Church of St. Lawrence, and other works too numerous to mention. Donatello, whose work to this hour is "all a wonder and a great desire;" Ghiberti, to whom Florence owes the gates of the Baptistery; Michelozzo, who built the Medici Palace and the Convent of San Marco, and was associated with Luca della Robbia in making the bronze gates of the Sacristy of the Duomo, belong to the same period, and were intimately associated with Brunelleschi in much of the work that makes Florence one of the show-places of the world to-day. Luca della Robbia was born when Fra Angelico was no more than twelve years old. Masolino, Masaccio, and Fra Filippo Lippi were among the painters of Fra Angelico's own time, while, when he was approaching middle age, Gian Bellini and Andrea Mantegna were growing up, and when Fra Angelico died, Florence was full of great artists who were destined to carry on his work. Of course, the literary activity was as great as the activity of the artists; one recalls with a thrill of emotion that Petrarch and Boccaccio were only just numbered among the dead – their work held all its earliest freshness. If at first sight these matters seem to be outside the scope of a brief consideration of Fra Angelico's life and work, second thought will justify the inclusion even in these narrow limits.

Every artist is in a sense an echo of his environment and, although Fra Angelico must have passed the greater part of his life within monastery walls, yet the evidence of his pictures must convince all who look with discerning eyes, that he was profoundly influenced by the life that went on around him. The artistic and literary movements of the time affected him deeply and, in his own modest way he was constantly striving to enlarge the boundaries of his art, to develop its achievements in a manner that must have made even his early pictures appear as dangerous as the works of artists like Manet and Degas seemed to their contemporaries. Had he lived in other times, had his lines been cast in some quiet city to which no echo of the new movement in art and letters could penetrate, Fra Angelico might still have painted interesting pictures; but he would not have got beyond his earliest manner, indeed he might not have attained to what is best in that. It would have been so very easy for a narrow-minded superior to say that the innovations were wrong, that the human figure in all its beauty must not be expressed by a painter when presenting Virgin and Child, that the old formal way was the right one. There could have been no appeal against such a judgment. Doubtless many a budding genius has been nipped in this fashion by short-sighted authority. How happy then was the friar with time and place united in his service.

VI

CONCLUSION

Fra Angelico has placed artists and laymen in his debt, and as far as the latter are concerned the cause is obvious enough. A certain conviction of the truth of every story he had to tell shines like a bright light through all his pictures; they are a force for the development and strengthening of belief. Even to-day one finds among the crowd of tourists that "does" San Marco in half-an-hour or more, a few visitors whose interest is of another kind, while there is no lack of admirers for the work to be seen in the Uffizi, though much of it belongs to the earliest part of the artist's life. So it happens that the pictures have a well-defined literary and spiritual value, and it is not surprising to think that the Church has granted posthumous honours to the man whose work has brought so much honour in its train. Artists acknowledge a great debt to the friar, but a debt of another kind. As Professor Langton Douglas has pointed out in his admirable and exhaustive work upon Fra Angelico, the friar, with his contemporaries, Hubert and Jan Van Eyck, are the fathers of modern landscape. The new movement was continued and developed by Verrocchio and Da

Vinci on the one side, and by Perugino and Raphael on the other. Then again Fra Angelico made a definite movement towards portrait painting, by giving the likeness of some of his friends and patrons to saints and martyrs. This was yet another of the daring innovations that marked the opening of the Quattrocento and, to realise how much it stood for we must consider for a moment the comparative barrenness of modern art, which in the hands of its most popular artists has little or nothing that is new to say to us. Indeed it may be remarked with regret that great praise often attaches to the man who goes back to the fifteenth and sixteenth century, although a little reflection would enable every thoughtful person to see that an art, forced to fall back upon traditions of the past, is far from being in a flourishing condition.

Illustrations of art by contemporaries of Fra Angelico on the following pages.

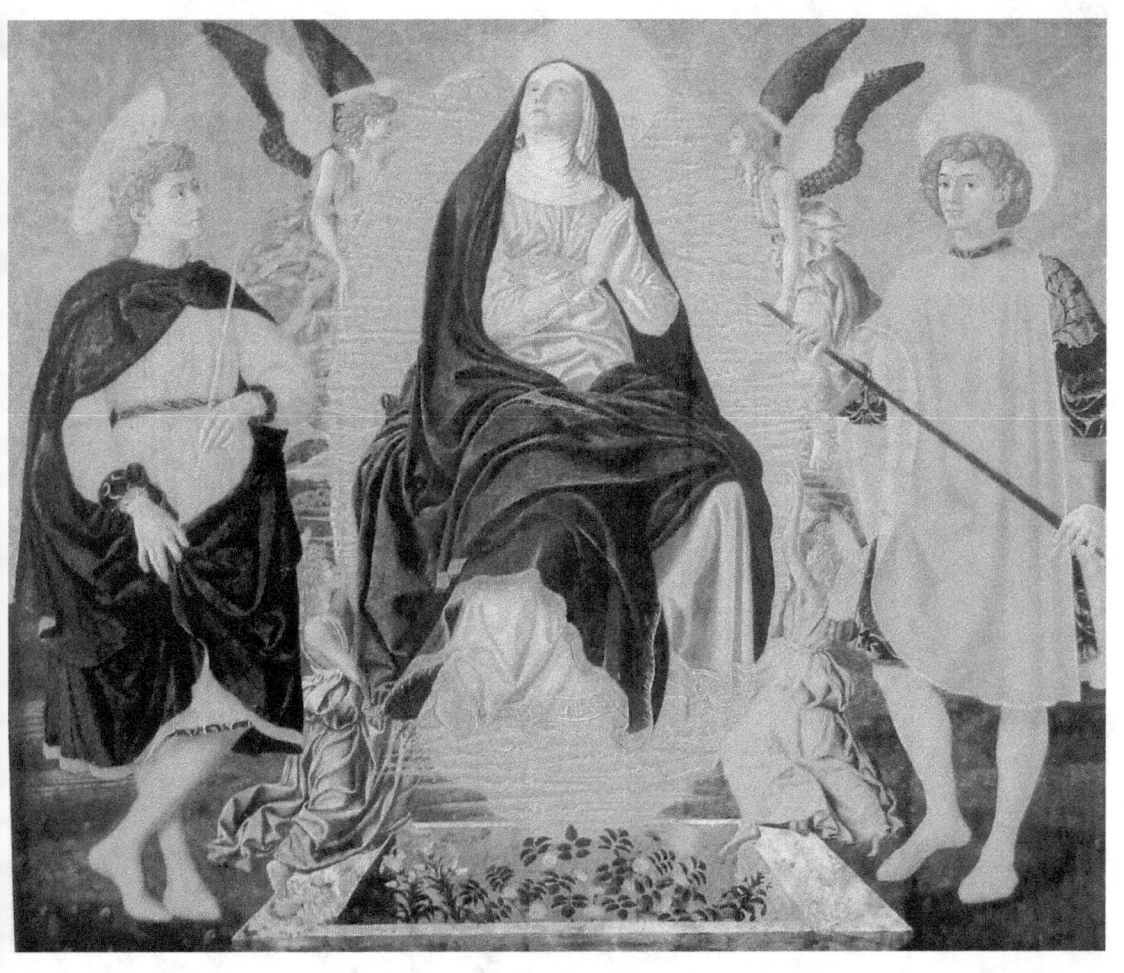

Andrea del Castagno, Assumption, Berlin

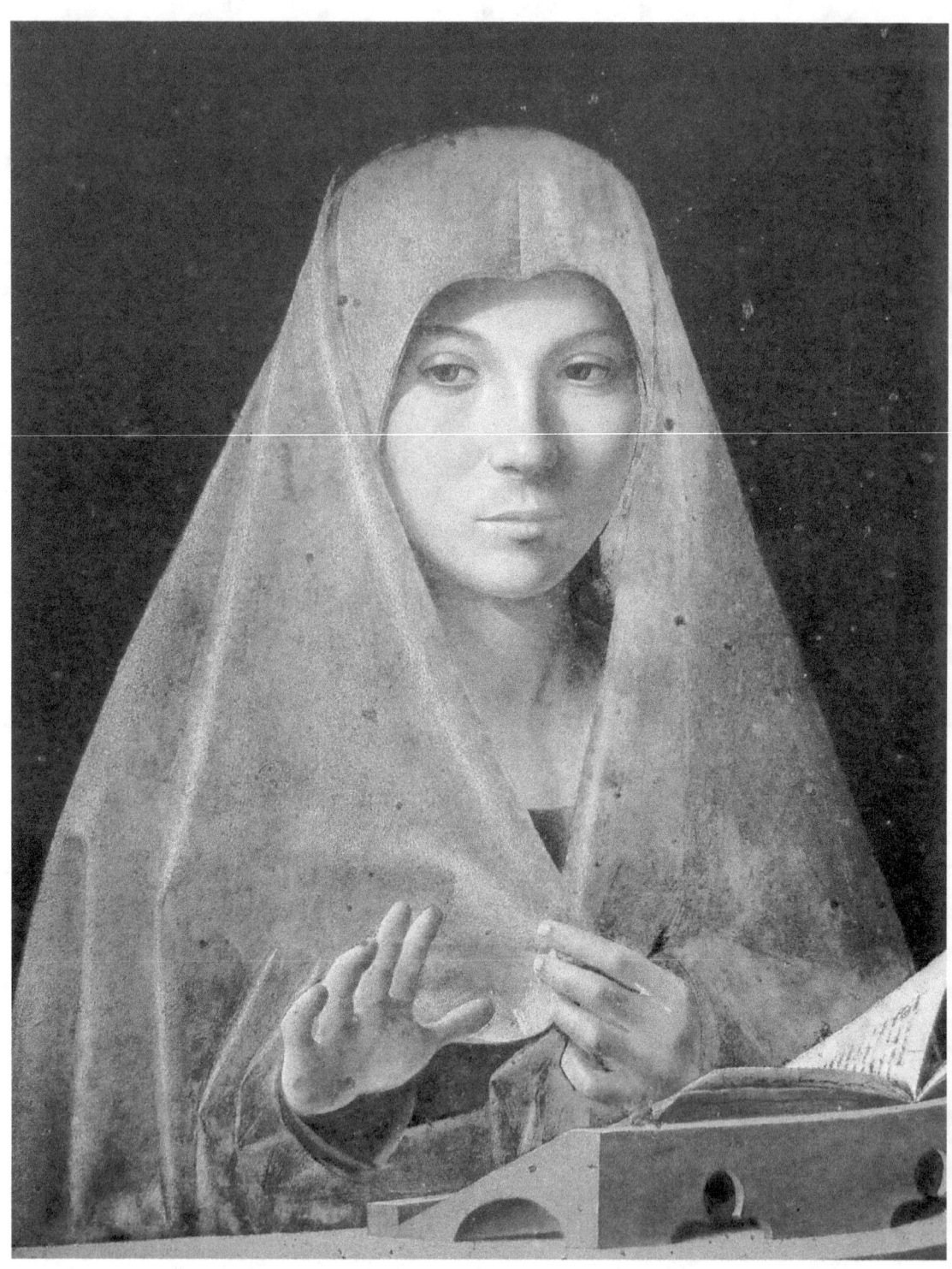

Antonello da Messina, The Virgin of the Annunciation, 1475, Palermo

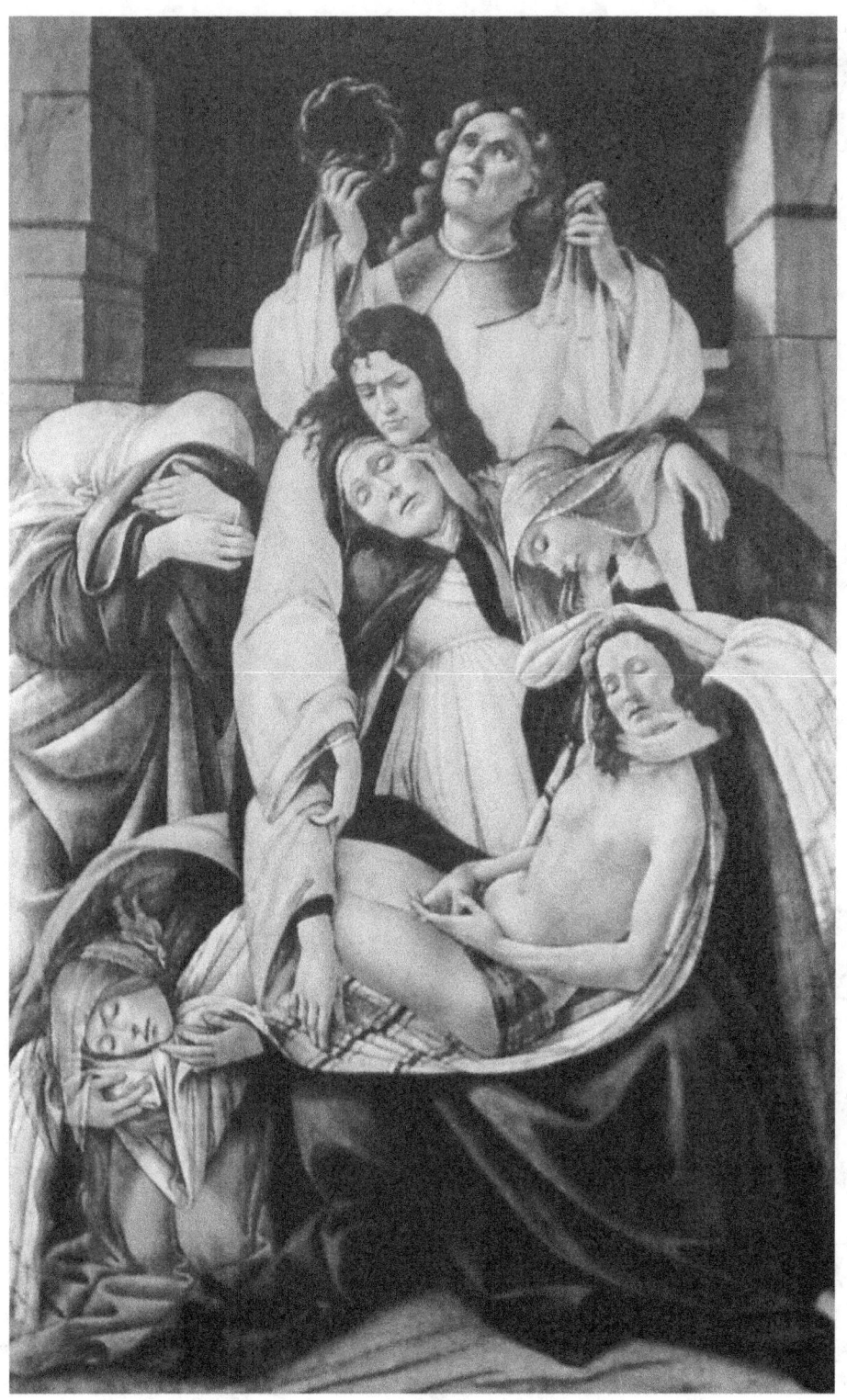

Sandro Botticelli, *Pietà*, Museo Poldi Pezzoli, Milan

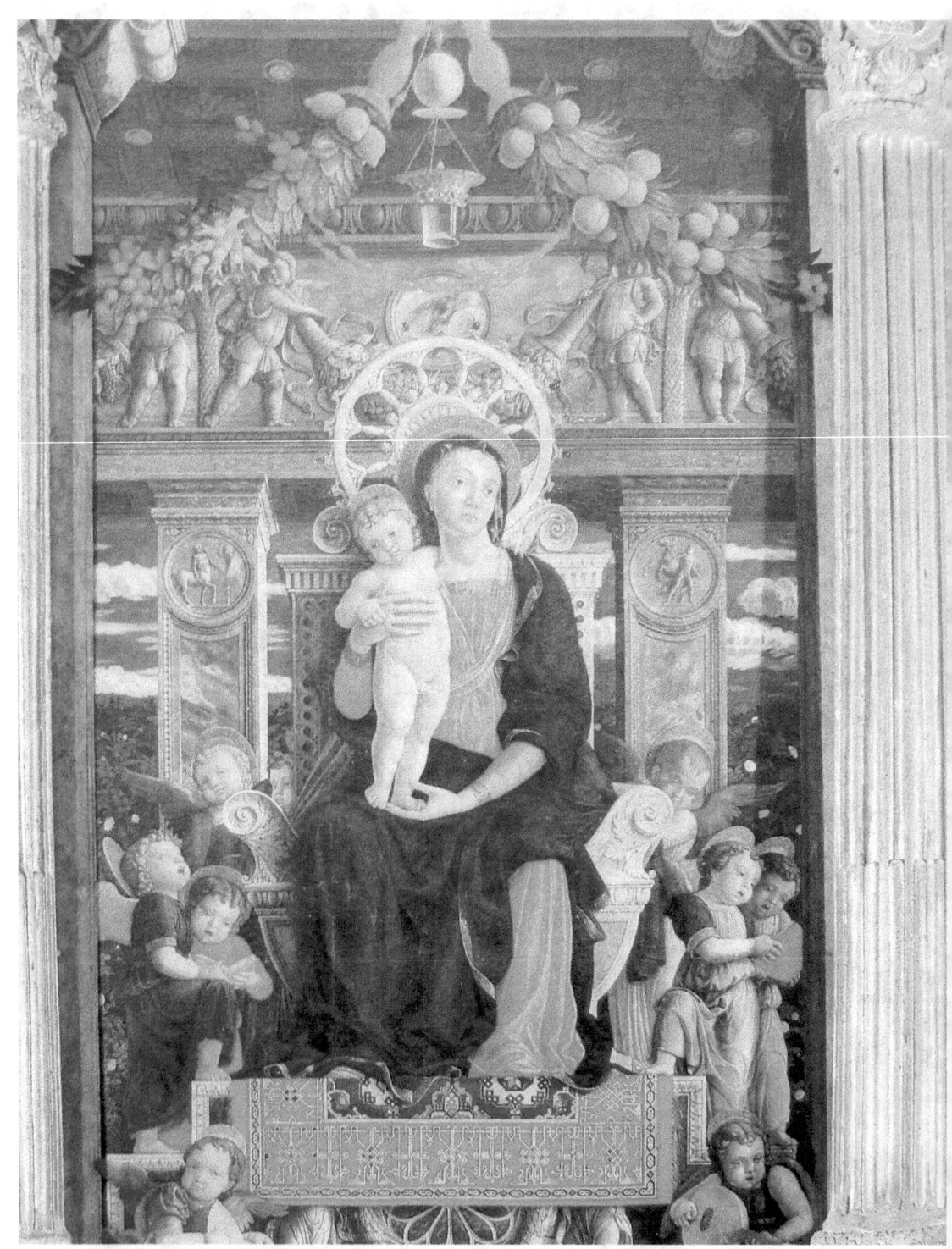

Andreas Mantegna, Madonna and Child Enthroned, 1457-60, Verona

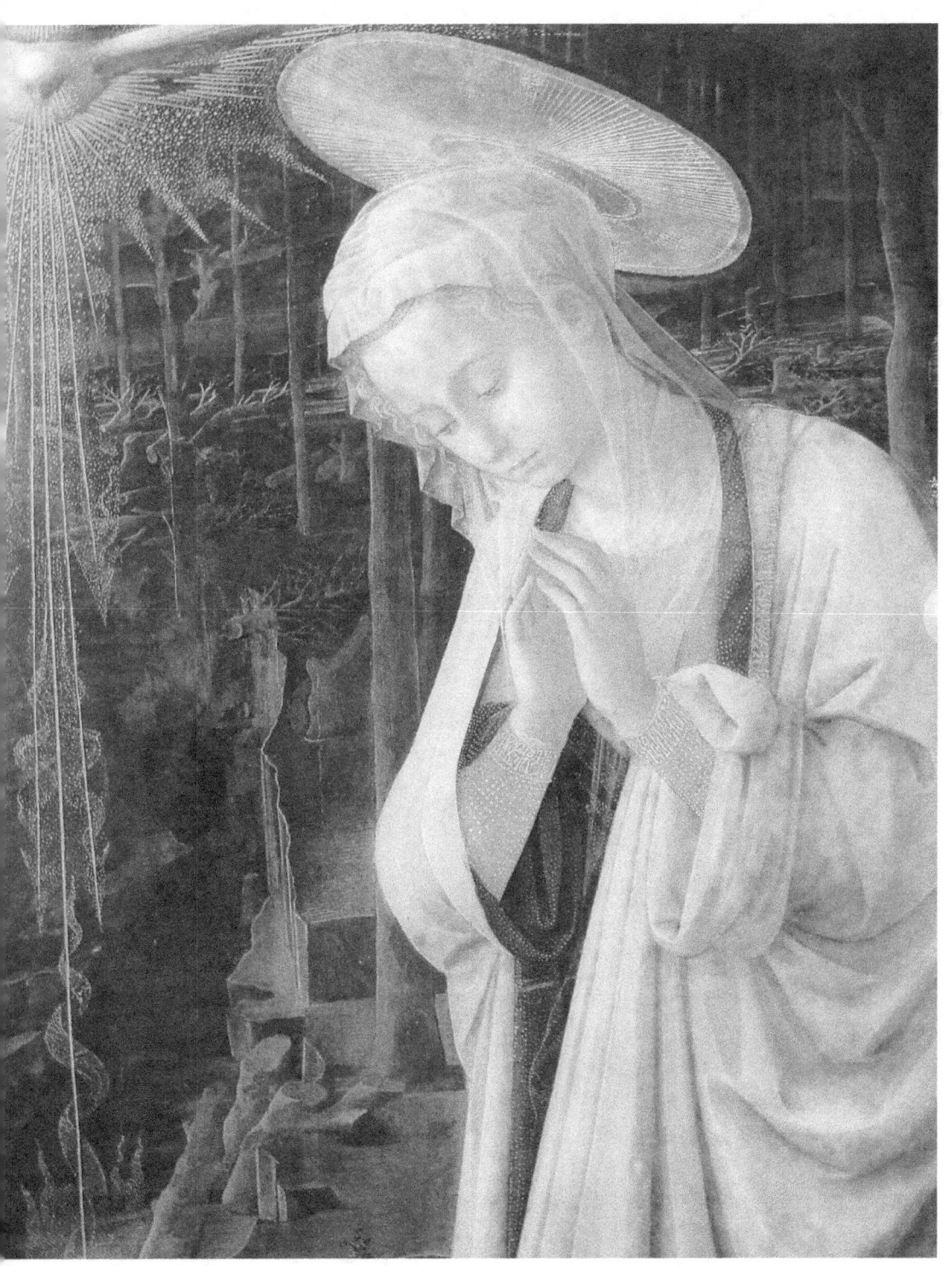

Fra Filippo Lippi, The Adoration of the Virgin, Berlin, detail

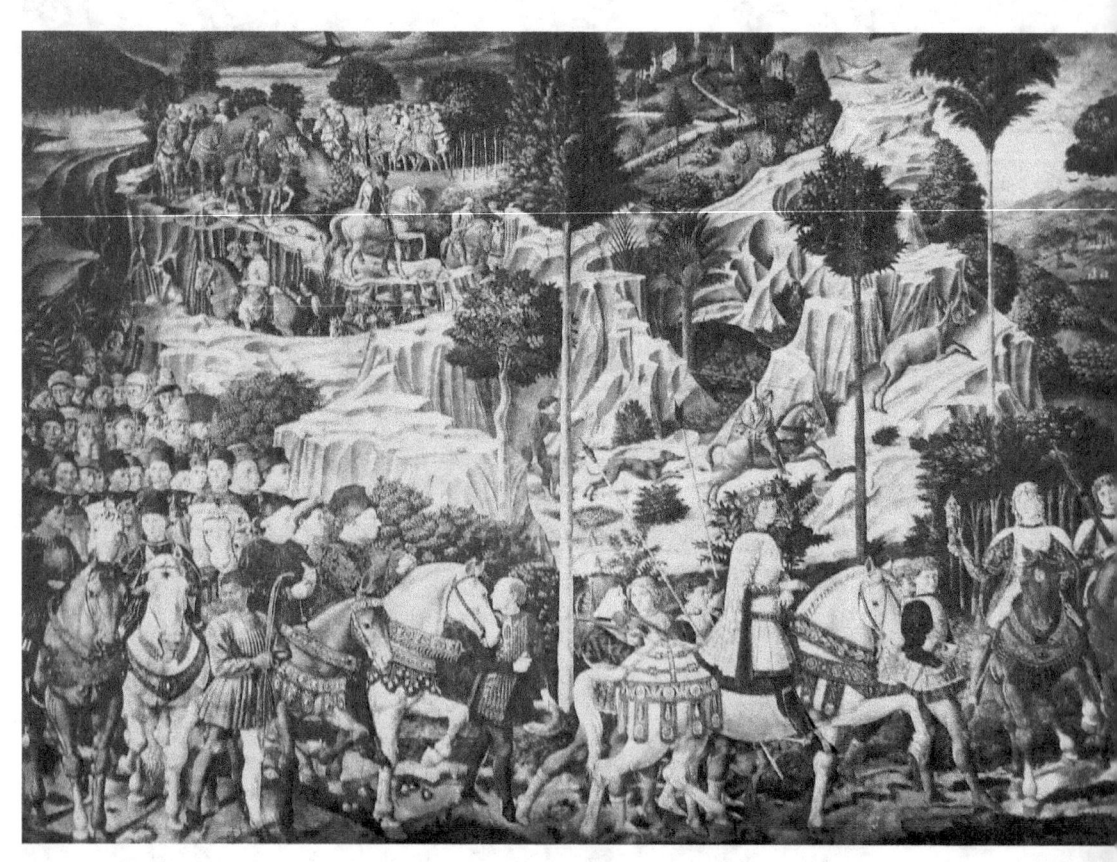

Benozzo Gozzoli, Journey of the Magi

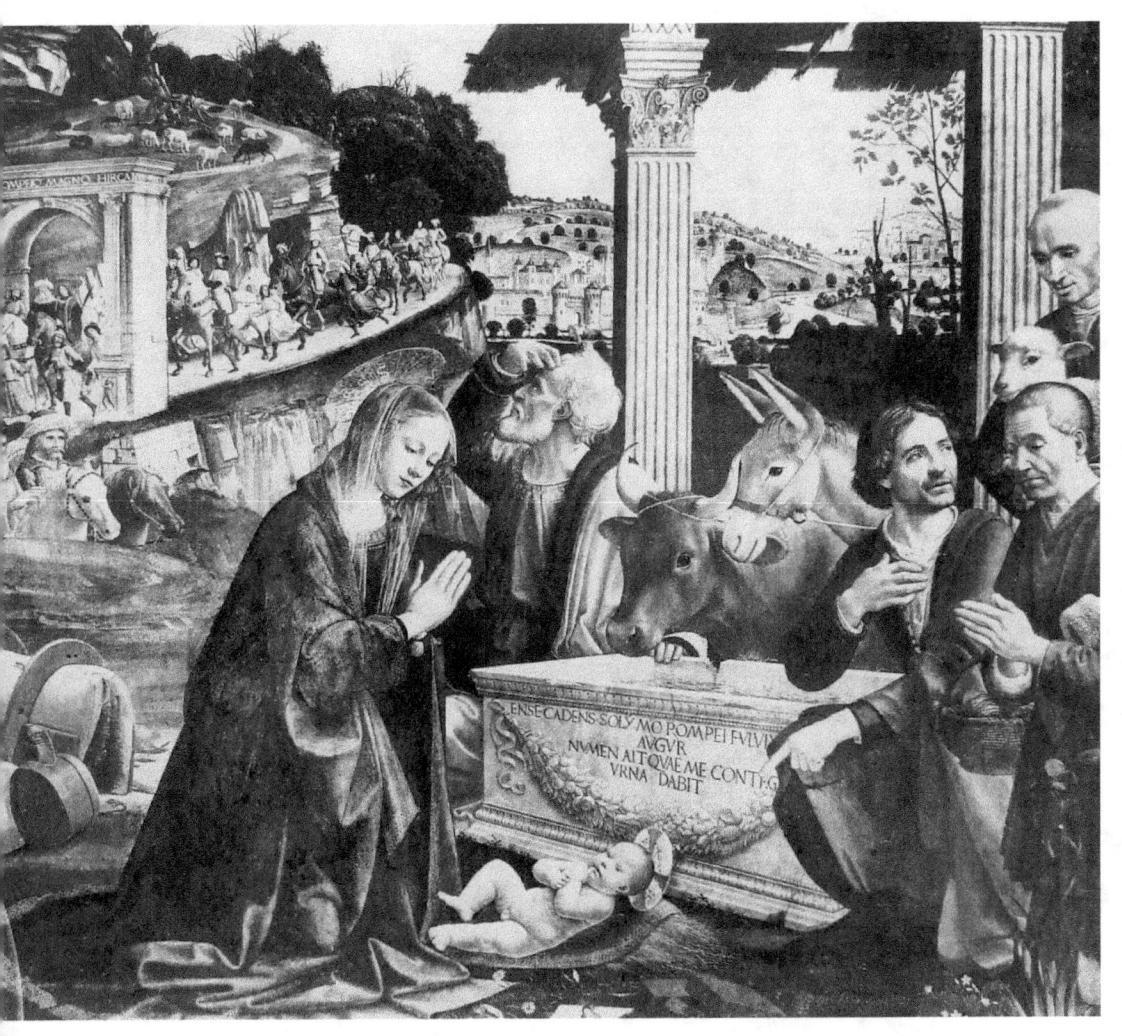

Domenico Ghirlandaio, Adoration of the Shepherds, 1485

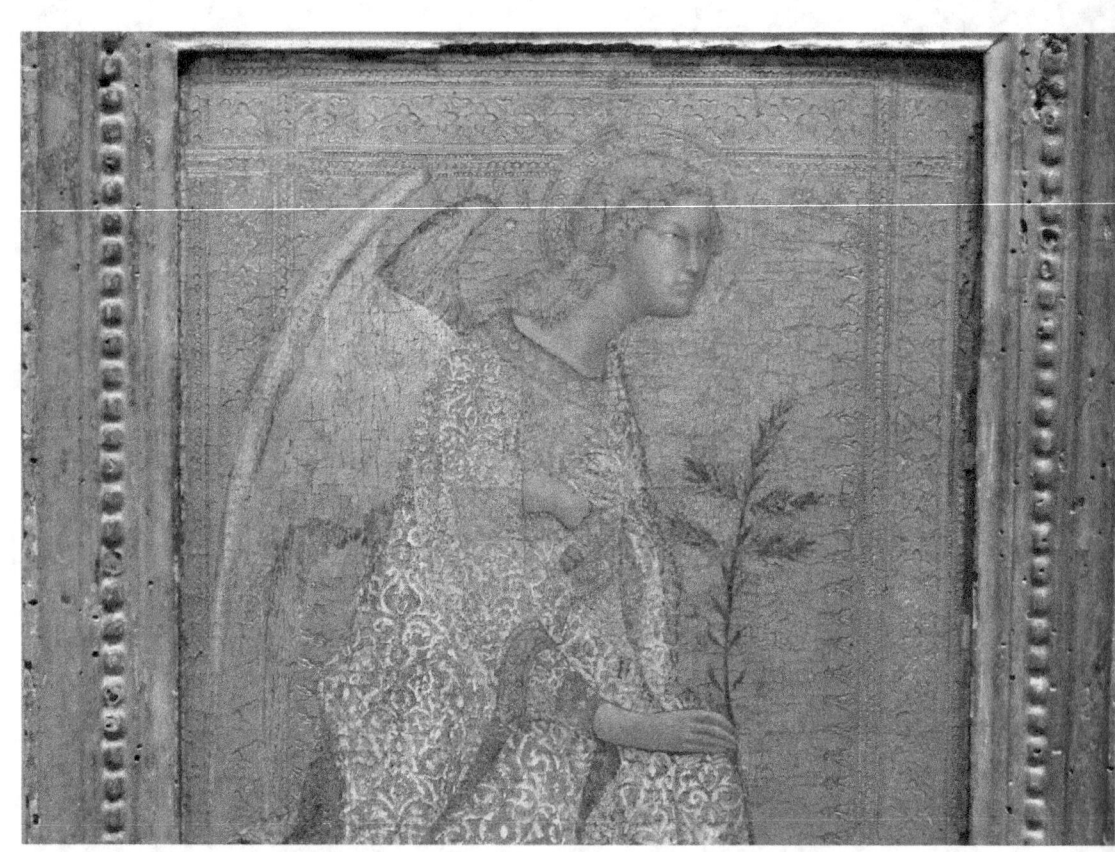

Simone Martini, Annunciation, Metropolitan Museum of Art, New York

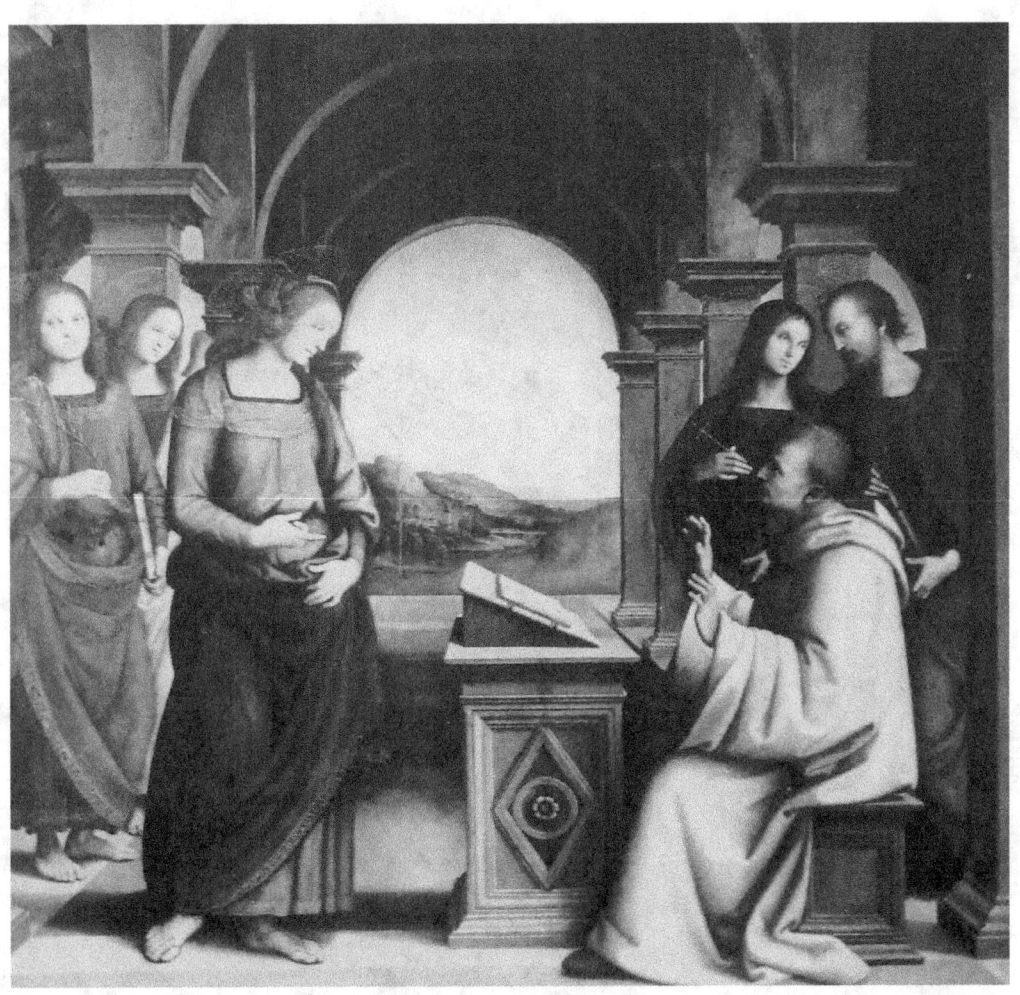

Perugino, Vision of St Bernard, 1488

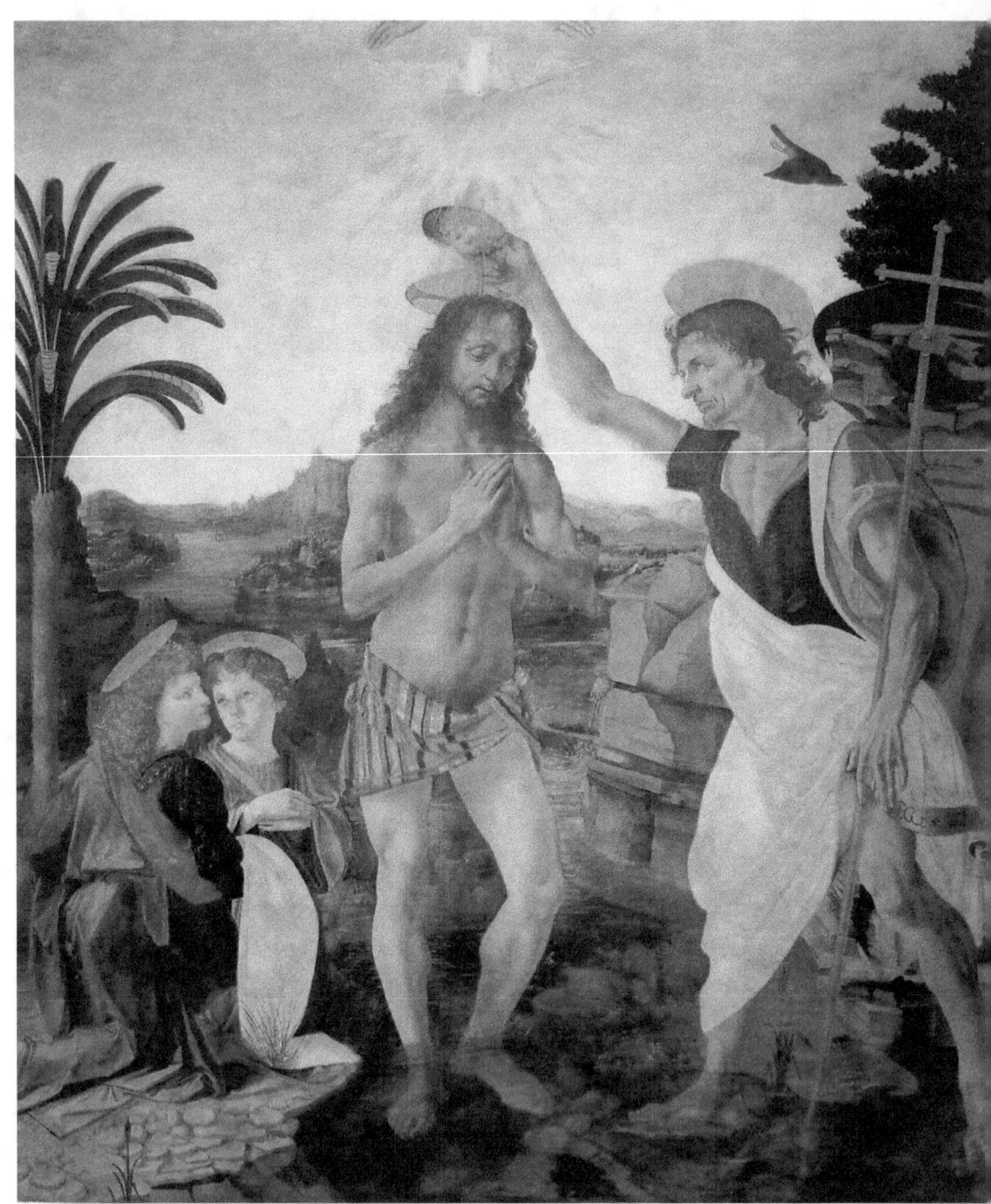

Andrea del Verrocchio, The Baptism of Christ

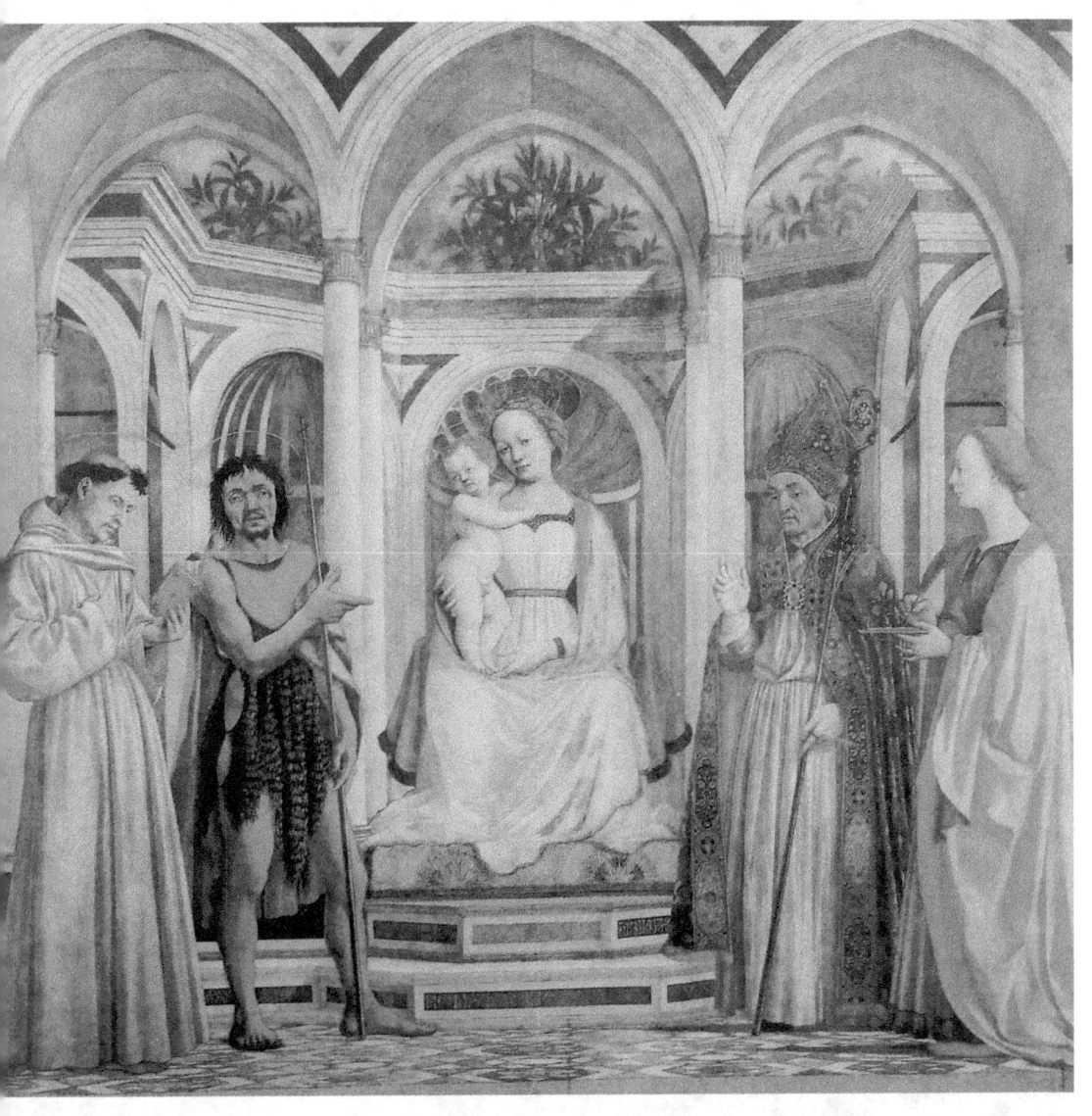

Domenico Veneziano, Madonna and Child With Saints, 1445, Uffizi Gallery

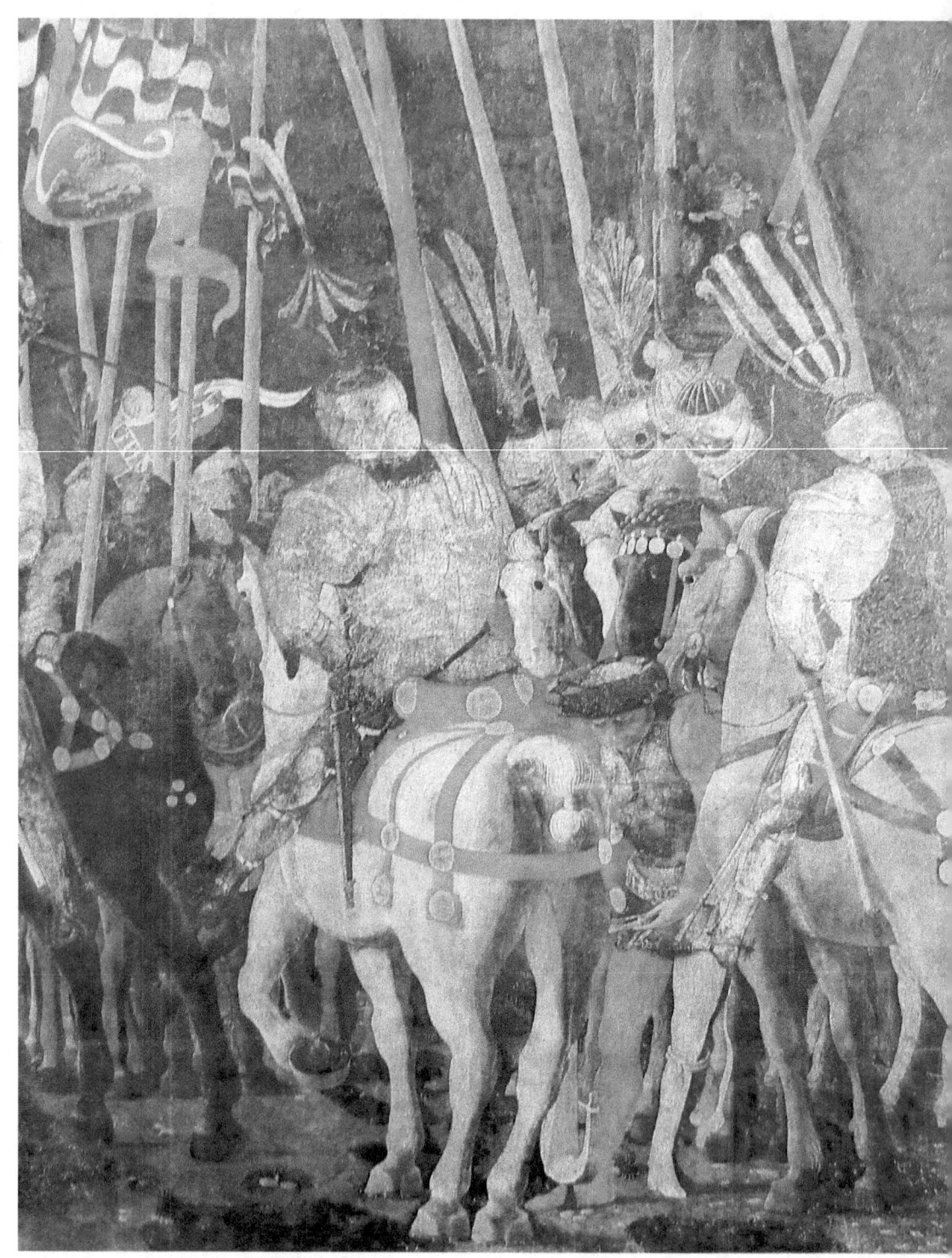

Paolo Uccello, Battle of San Romano, 1456-60, Loure, Paris

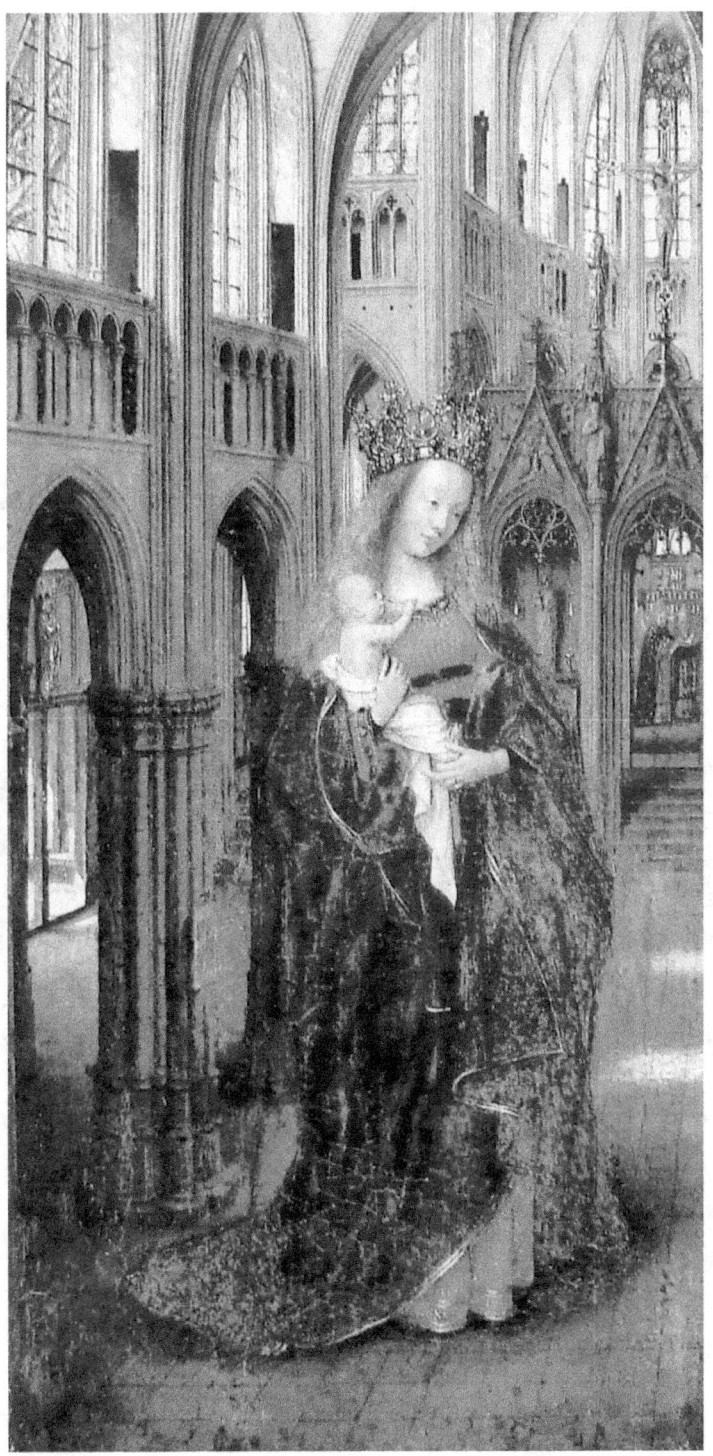

Jan van Eyck, Madonna In a Church, Berlin

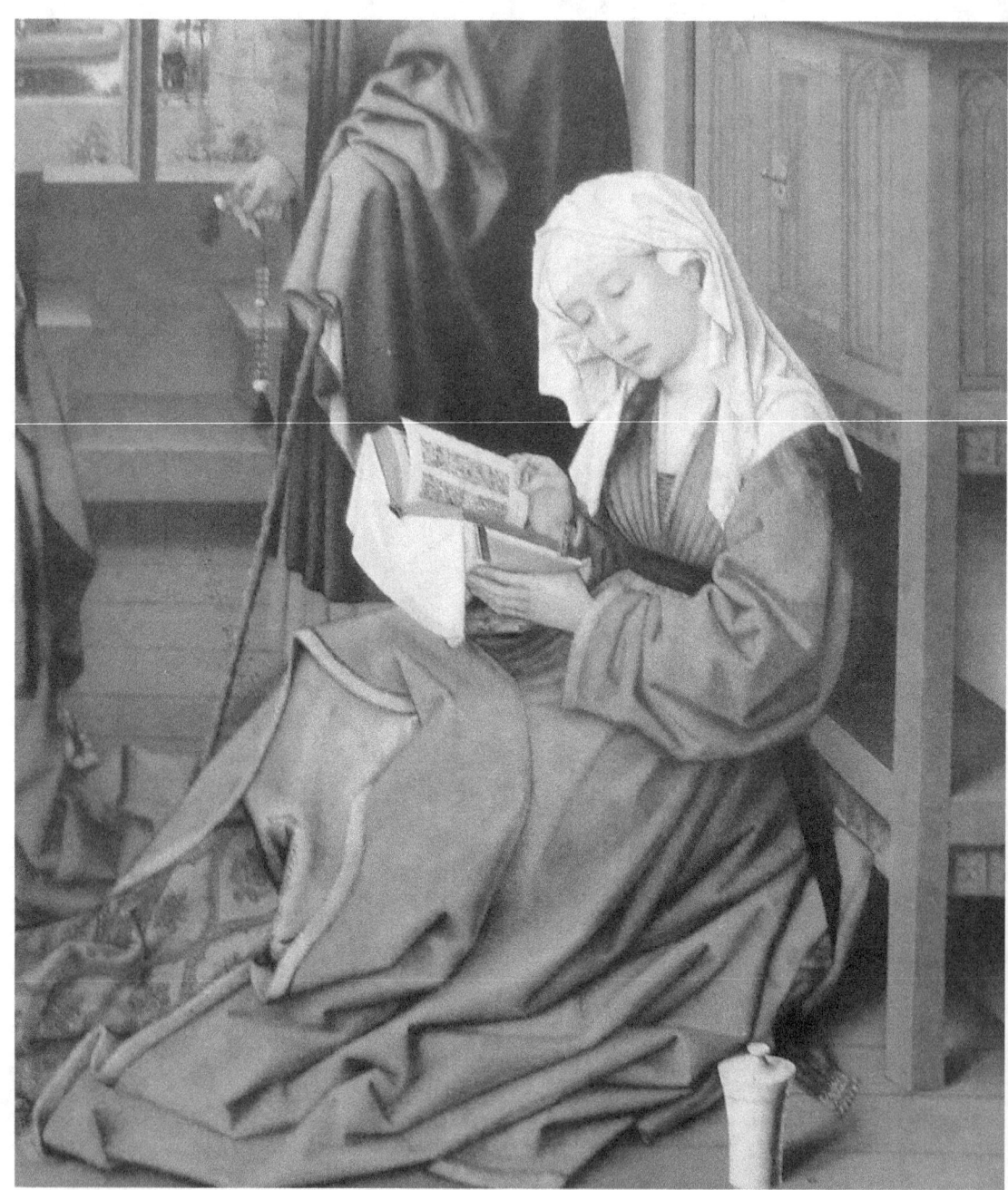

Rogier van der Weyden, Mary Magdalene Reading, detail, National Gallery, London

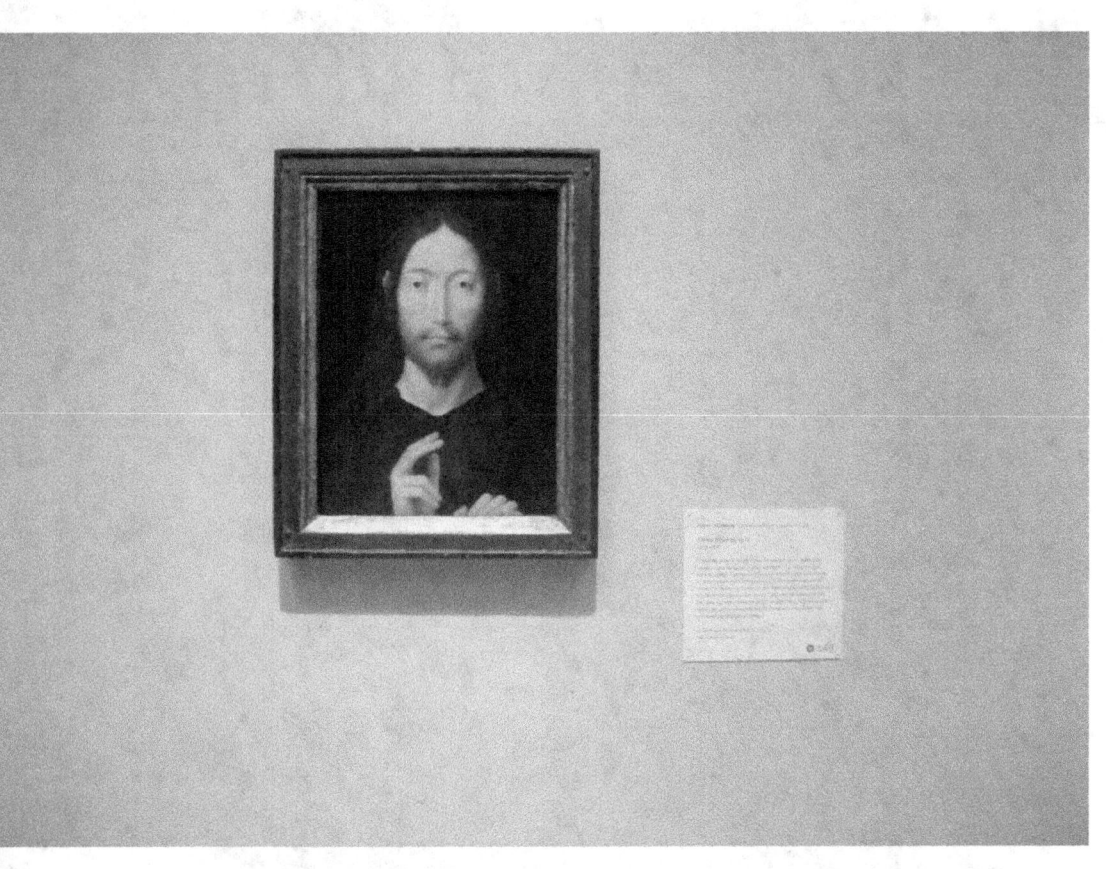

Hans Memling, Christ Blessing, Metropolitan Museum of Art

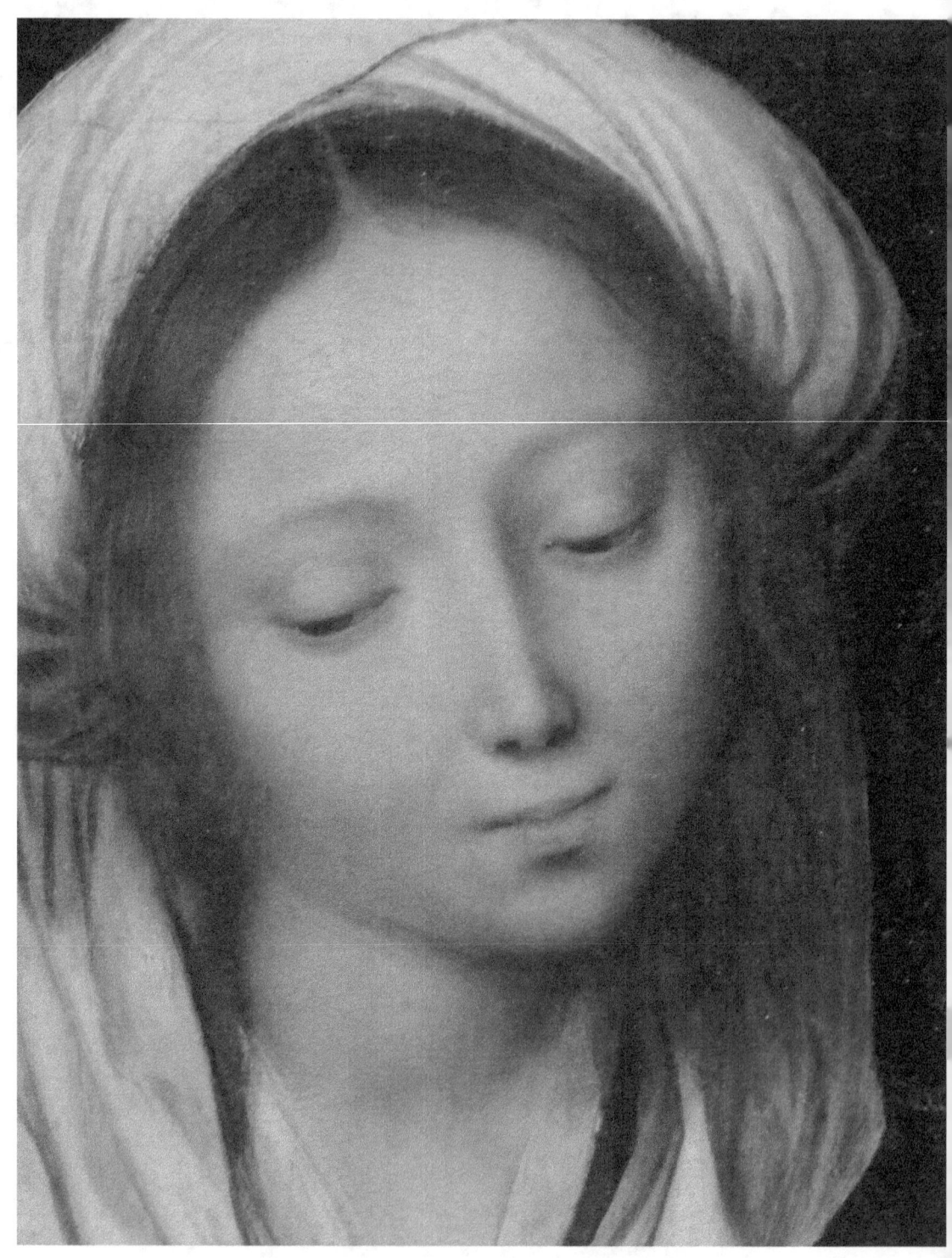

Gerard David, detail of the Adoration, Metropolitan Museum of Art

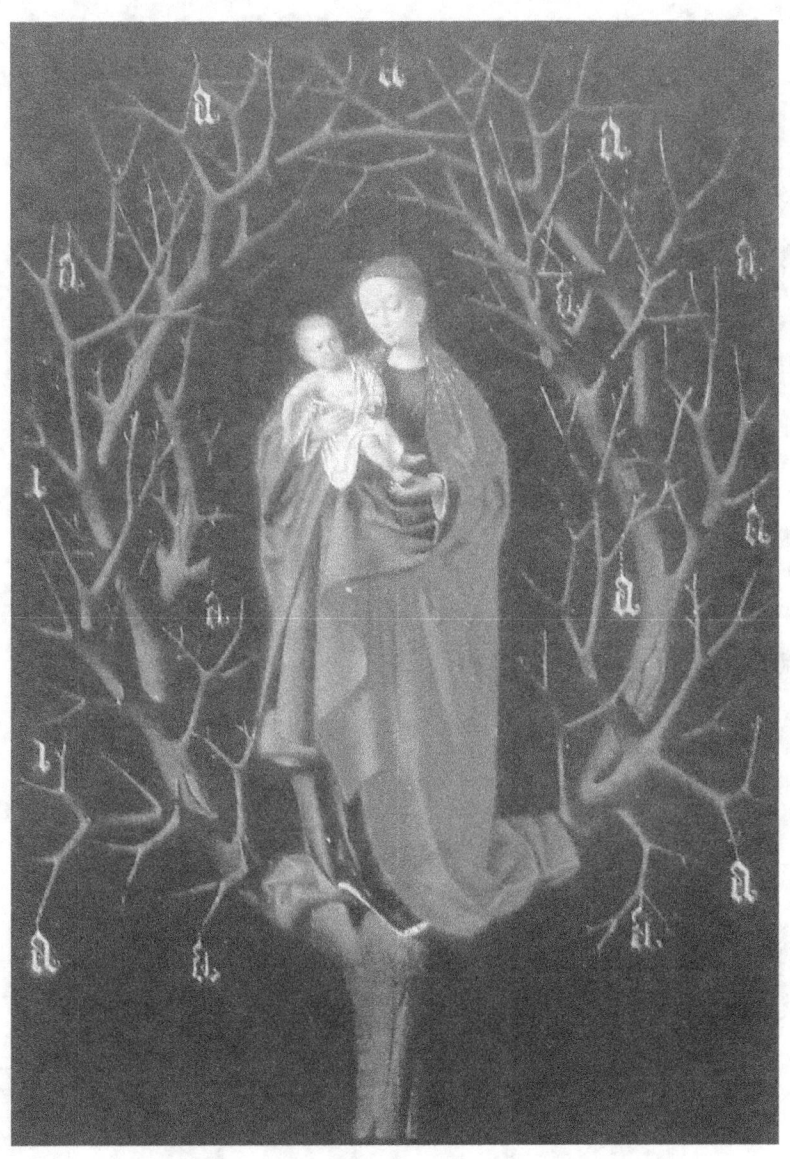

Petrus Christus, Madonna In a Barren Tree, 1450,
Prado, Madrid

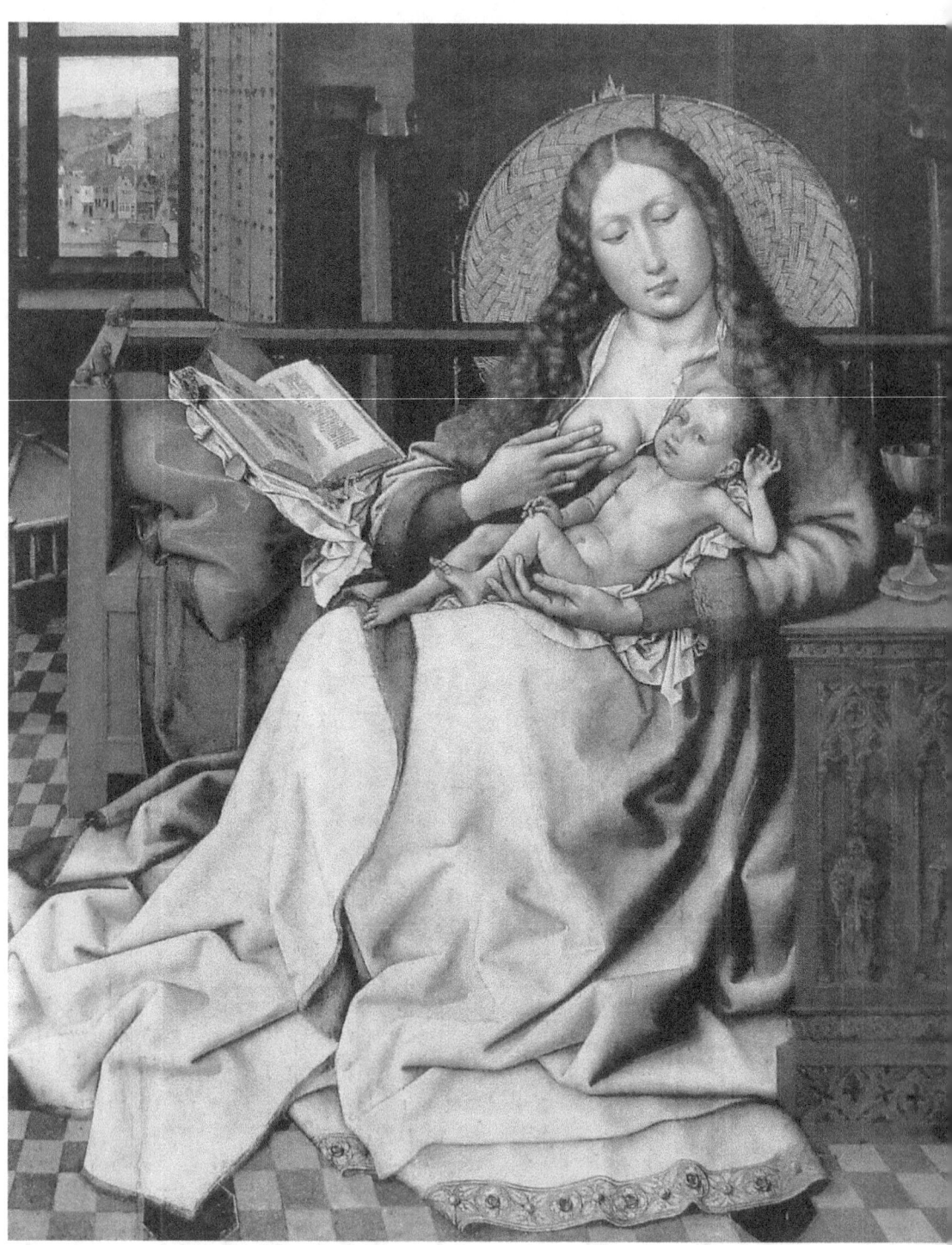

Robert Campin, Madonna With the Firescreen, National Gallery, London

BIBLIOGRAPHY[1]

I   *Fra Angelico*

C. Argan: *Fra Angelico*, Skira, Geneva 1955

U. Baldini: *Beato Angelico*, Edizioni d'Arte il Fiorino, Florence 1986

L. Berti et al: *Angelico at San Marco*, Sansoni, Florence 1965

M. OskovitsL "La fase tarda del Beato Angelico", *Arte cristiana*, LXXI, 1983, 11-24

—"Arte e formazione religosa – Il caso del Beato Angelico", in *L'uomo di fronte all'arte. Valori estetici e valori etico-religiosi*, La Spezia, 1985, *Vita e Pensiero*, 1986, 153-164

P. Cardile: "Fra Angelico's Shop at San Domenico in Fiesole", Ph. D thesis, Yale University 1974

G. Didi-Huberman: *Fra Angelico. Dissemblance et Figuration*, Flammarion, Paris 1990

—"La dissemblance des figures selon Fra Angelico", *Mélanges de l'Ecole Française de Rome. Moyn Age – Temps Moderne*, XCVIII, 1986, 709-802

D. Dini & G. Bonsanti: "Fra Angelico e gli affreschi nel Convento di San Marco (ca. 1441-50)", in E. Borsook & F. Superbi Gioffredi, ed: *Tecnica e Stile. Esempi di pittura murale del Rinascimento italiano*, Harvard Center for Italian Renaissance Studies at Villa I Tatti, 1986, 17-24

A. Francini Ciaranfi: *Beato Angelico: Gli affreschi di San Marco*, Amilcare Pizzi S. p. A, Milan 1940

C. Gilbert: "A Sign about Signing in a Fresco by Fra Angelico", in *Tribute to Lotte Brand Phi;lip*, Abaris Books, New York 1985, 65-70

—"Fra Angeloc", *Theologische Realenzyklopädie*, II, 5, Waler de Gruyter, Berlin, 19978, 710-3

1 From *Fra Angelico* by Rosalind Mutter, Crescent Moon, 2008.

—"The Conversion of Fra Angelico", in *Scritti di Storia dell'Arte in onore di Roberto Salvini*, ed. C. De Benedictis, G.C. Sansoni Editore Nuova, Florence 1984, 281-7

A. Hertz: *Fra Angelico,* Edizioni Paoline, Rome 1983

William Hood: *Fra Angelico at San Marco,* Yale University Press, New Haven 1993

—"Fra Angelico at San Marco: Art and the Liturgy of Cloistered Life", in T. Verdon & J. Henderson, eds: *Christianity and the Renaissance,* Syracuse University Press, Syracuse 1990, 108-131

—"St Dominic's Manners of Praying: Gestures in Fra Angelico's Frescoes at S. Marco", *Art bulletin,* LXVIII, 1986, 195-206

P. Joannides: "Fra Angelico: Two Annunciations", *Arte cristiana,* LXXVII, 1989, 303-308

R. Krautheimer: "Fra Angelico and – perhaps – Alberti", in J. Plummer & I. Lavin, eds: *Studies in Late Medieval and Renaissance Painting Presented to Millard Meiss,* New York University Press, New York 1977, 290-296

A. Ladis: "Fra Angelico: newly discovered document from the 1420s", *Mitteilungen des Kunsthistorischen Institutes in Florenz,* XXV, 1981, 378-9

Christopher Lloyd: *Fra Angelico,* Phaidon 1979

S. Madigan: "A New Interpretation of the Iconography of Fra Angelico: Rosarian Organization in the Frescoed Cells of San Marco", MACAA paper, Hamlite University, St Paul, 1977

J. Miller: "Medici Patronage and the Iconography of Fra Angelico's San Marco Altarpiece", *Studies in Iconography,* XI, 1987, 1-13

S. Orlandi: *Beato Angelico,* Leo S. Olscki, Florence 1964

John Pope-Hennessy: *Fra Angelico,* Phaidon 1974

U. Procacci: "Recent restoration in Florence, II: Fra Angelico, Sassetta and others", *Burlington Magazine,* LXXXIX, 1947, 330-4

M. Salmi: *Beato Angelico,* Edizioni Valori Plastici, Rome 1958

P. Sheaffer: "White Light and Meditation at San Marco", *Memorie Domenicane,* XIV, 1983, 329-334

I. Strunk: *Fra Angelico aus dem Dominikanerorden,* B. Kuehlens Kunstanstalt u. Verlag, Gladbach 1916

C.G. Argan: *The Renaissance*, Thames & Hudson 1969

Karen Armstrong: *The Gospel According to Woman; Christianity's Creation of the Sex War in the West*, Pan 1987

Karen Arthurs: *A Survey of the Notions Behind, and the Mechanics of, Harmony Within the Composition of Art From Prehistory to the Renaissance*, BA thesis, Newcastle Polytechnic 1984

Geoffrey Ashe: *The Virgin: Mary's Cult and the Re-emergence of the Goddess*, Arkana 1987

—*Discovering the Goddess: A Personal Testimony*, Crescent Moon 1995

Michael Baxandall: *Painting and Experience in 15th Century Italy*, Oxford University Press 1988

—*Patterns of Intention: On the Historical Explanation of Pictures*, Yale University Press 1985

James Beck: *Italian Renaissance Painting*, Harper & Row, New York 1981

Ean Begg: *The Cult of the Black Virgin*, Routledge 1985

Bernard Berenson: *The Italian Painters of the Renaissance*, Phaidon 1952

—*Looking at Pictures with Bernard Berenson*, selected by Hann Kiel, Abrahams, New York 1974

Pamela Berger: *The Goddess Obscured*, Robert Hale 1988

Bruce Bernard: *The Queen of Heaven: A Selection of Painting the Virgin from the Twelfth to the Eighteenth Centuries*, Macdonald/ Orbis 1987

—*The Bible and Its Painters*, Orbis 1983

Botticelli: *The Complete Paintings of Botticelli*, Granada 1980

Charles Bouleau: *The Painter's Secret Geometry: A Study of Composition in Art*, tr Jonathan Griffin, Thames & Hudson 1963

Serge Bramly: *Leonardo: The Artist and the Man*, Michael Joseph 1992

Allan Brahama: *Italian Renaissance Painters of the Sixteenth Century*, National Gallery 1985

Helmut Brinker: *Zen in the Art of Painting*, Routledge & Kegan Paul 1987

Stephanie Brown: *Religious Painting*, Phaidon 1979

Jacob Burckhardt: *The Altarpiece in Renaissance Italy*, Phaidon 1988

Titus Burckhardt: *Sacred Art in East and West*, Perennial Book, Middlesex 1967

Ritchie Calder: *Leonardo and The Age of the Eye*, Heinemann 1970

Joseph Campbell: *The Power of Myth*, with Bill Moyers, ed. Betty Sue Flowers, Doubleday, New York 1988

Michael P. Carroll: *The Cult of the Virgin Mary*, Princeton University

Press, New Jersey 1986

Richard Cavendish: *Visions of Heaven and Hell*, Orbis 1977

Andre Chastel: *Art of the Italian Renaissance*, tr Peter & Linda Murray, Alpine Fine Arts Collection 1985

— *The Studios and Styles of the Renaissance, Italy 1460-1500*, tr Griffin, Thames & Hudson 1966

Herschel B. Chipp, ed. *Theories of Modern Art*, University Press of California, Los Angeles 1968

Bruce Cole: *The Renaissance Artist at Work*, John Murray 1983

Charles D. Cuttler: *Northern Painting From Pucelle to Bruegel*, Holt, Rineheart & Winston, New York 1968

Lene Dresen-Coenders, ed: *Saints and She-Devils: Images of Women in the 15th and 16th Centuries*, Rubicon Press 1987

Steven C. Dubin: *Arresting Images: Impolitic Art and Uncivil Actions*, Routledge 1992

Andrea Dworkin: *Intercourse*, Arrow 1988

— *Pornography: Men Possessing Women*, Women's Press 1984

Donald Ehresmann: "Some Observations on the Role of the Liturgy in the Early Winged Altarpiece", *Art Bulletin*, LXIV, 1982

Colin Eisler: *Early Netherlandish Painting: The Thyssen-Bornemisza Collection*, Sotheby's Publications 1989

Mircea Eliade: *Ordeal by Labyrinth*, University of Chicago Press 1984

— *Symbolism, the Sacred and the Arts*, Crossroad, New York 1985

Joan Evans, ed: *The Flowering of the Middle Ages*, Thames & Hudson 1966

Giorgio T. Faggin: *The Complete Paintings of the Van Eycks*, Wiedenfeld & Nicolson 1970

John Fletcher & Andrew Benjamin, ed; *Abjection, Melancholia and Love: the Work of Julia Kristeva*, Routledge 1990

S.J. Freedberg: *Painting of the High Renaissance in Rome and Florence*, Harper & Row, New York 1972

Sigmund Freud: *Leonardo da Vinci*, tr Alan Tyson, Penguin 1963

Max J. Friedlander: *From Van Eyck to Bruegel*, Phaidon 1969

— *The van Eycks, Petrus Christus*, Early Netherlandish Painting vol. 1, tr Heinz Norden, Sijthoff, Leyden, Netherlands 1967

Eugène Fromentin: *The Masters of Past Time: Dutch and Flemish Painting from Van Eyck to Rembrandt*, Phaidon 1981

Niny Garavaghlia: *The Complete Paintings of Mantegna*, Weidenfeld & Nicholson 1971

Fred Gettings: *The Hidden Art: A Study of the Occult Symbolism in Art*, Studio Vista 1978

Matila Ghyka: *The Geometry of Art and Life*, Sheed & Ward, New York

1946

Marija Gimbutas: *The Language of the Goddess*, Thames & Hudson 1989

Rona Goffen: *Giovanni Bellini*, Yale University Press, New Haven 1989

Robert Goldwater & Marco Treves, eds. *Artists on Art*, John Murray 1975

E.H. Gombrich: *Norm and Form: Studies in the Renaissance I*, Phaidon 1985
— *Symbolic Images, Renaissance Studies II*, Phaidon 1985

Cecil Gould: *Leonardo: The Artist and the Non-Artist*, Weidenfeld &
   Nicholson 1975

— "On the Direction of Light in Italian Renaissance Frescoes and
   Altarpieces", *Gazette des Beaux-Arts*, 6, XCVII, 1981

John Hale: *Italian Renaissance Painting*, Phaidon 1977

James Hall: *A Dictionary of Subjects and Symbols in Art*, John Murray 1984

Frederick Hartt: *History of Italian Renaissance Art: Painting, Sculpture,
   Architecture*, Thomas & Hudson 1987

— *Sandro Botticelli*, Collins 1954

P. Jolly: "Rogier van der Weyden's Escorial and Philadelphia *Crucifixions*
   and their relation to Fra Angelico at San Marco", *Oud Holland*, XCV,
   1981, 113-126

Julia Kristeva: *The Kristeva Reader*, ed Toril Moi, Blackwell 1986

— *Desire in Language: A Semiotic Approach to Literature and Art*, ed Leon
   Roudiez, tr Thomas Gora, Alice Jardine & Leon Roudiez, Blackwell
   1982

Weston La Barre: *The Ghost Dance*, Allen & Unwin 1972

Barbara Lane: *The Altar and the Altarpiece: Sacramental Themes in Early
   Netherlandish Painting*, New York 1984

— "Sacred vs Profane in Early Netherlandish Painting", *Simiolus*, XVIII,
   1988

Leonardo da Vinci: *The Drawings of Leonardo da Vinci*, introduction A.E.
   Popham, Cape, 1964

— *Selections from the Notebooks*, Oxford University Press 1952

Michael Levey: *High Renaissance*, Penguin 1975

— *Early Renaissance*, Penguin 1967

Robert Longhi: *Piero della Francesca*, Milan 1955

Emile Male: *The Gothic Image*, Collins 1961

Elaine Marks & Isabelle de Courtivron, eds: *New French Feminisms: an
   Anthology*, Harvester Wheatsheaf 1981

G. Marchini: *Filippo Lippi*, Electa Editrice, Milan 1975

James Marrow: "Symbol and Meaning in Northern European Art of the
   Late Middle Ages and Early Renaissance", *Simiolus*, XVI, 1986

Milliard Meiss: "Light as Form and Symbol in Some Fifteenth Century
   Paintings", *Art Bulletin*, XXVII, 1945

J.C.J. Metford: *Dictionary of Christian Lore and Legend,* Thames & Hudson 1983

Edward Mullins: *The Painted Witch: Female Body, Male Art,* Secker & Warburg 1985

Peter & Linda Murray: *The Penguin Dictionary of Art and Artists,* Penguin 1976

Linda Murray: *High Renaissance,* Thames & Hudson 1977

Lynda Nead: *Female Nude: Art, Obscenity and Sexuality,* Routledge 1992

Erich Neumann: *The Great Mother,* Princeton University Press, New Jersey 1972

Shirley Nicholson, ed. *The Goddess Re-awakening: The Goddess Principle Today* Theosophical Publishing House, New York 1989

Rudolf Otto: *The Idea of the Holy,* Oxford University Press 1958

Erwin Panofsky: *Studies in Iconology,* Harper & Row, New York 1972

—*Early Netherlandish Painting,* Harvard University Press, Mass., 1953

Walter Pater: *The Renaissance,* Oxford University Press 1980

Michael Payne: *Reading Theory: An Introduction to Lacan, Derrida, and Kristeva,* Blackwell 1993

Robert Payne: *Leonardo da Vinci,* Robert hale 1979

Lotte Brand Philip: *The Ghent Altarpiece and the Art of Jan van Eyck,* Princeton University Press 1971

C. Purtle: *The Marian Paintings of Jan van Eyck,* Princeton University Press, Princeton 1982

Kathleen J. Reiger, ed: *The Spiritual Image in Modern Art,* Theosophical Publ-ishing House, Wheaton, Illinois 1987

D. Robb: "The Iconography of the Annunciation in the Fourteenth and Fifteenth Centuries", *Art Bulletin,* XVIII, 1936, 480-526

John Ruskin: *Works,* ed. E.T.Cook & A. Wedderburn, 39 vols, Allen 1903-12

Monica Sjöo & Barbara Mor: *The Great Cosmic Mother,* Harper & Row, San Francisco 1987

Alistair Smith: *Early Netherlandish and German Painting,* National Gallery 1985

J. Spencer: "Spatial Imagery of the Annunciation in Fifteenth-century Flor-ence", *Art Bulletin,* XXXVI, 1955, 273-280

Oswald Spengler: *The Decline of the West,* Allen & Unwin 1961

Wolfgang Stechow: *Northern Renaissance Art, 1400-1600, Sources and Documents,* Prentice-Hall, New Jersey 1966

L. Steinberg & S. Edgerton: "How shall this be? Reflections on Filippo Lippi's *Annunciation* in London", *Artibus et Historiæ,* VIII, 1987, 25-53

Victor I. Stoichita: *Leonardo da Vinci,* Abbey Library 1978

Nicholas Usherwood: *The Bible in 20th Century Art*, Pagoda Books 1987

Lionello Venturi: *Renaissance Painting, from Leonardo to Dürer*, Skira/ Macmillan 1979

— *Italian Paintings*, Zwemmer 1950

— *Botticelli*, Phaidon 1964

Marina Warner: *Alone Of All Her Sex: The Myth and Cult of the Virgin Mary*, Picador 1985

— *Monuments and Maidens*, Weidenfeld & Nicholson 1985

Margaret Whinney: *Early Flemish Painters*, Faber 1966

John White: *The Birth and Rebirth of Pictorial Space*, Faber 1957/87

Peter Lamborn Wilson: *Angels*, Thames & Hudson 1980

Heinrich Wolfflin: *Classic Art*, Phaidon 1952/80

Marion Woodman: *The Pregnant Virgin: A Process of Psychological Transformation*, Inner City Books, Toronto 1989

Manfred Wudram: *Art of the Renaissance*, Weidenfeld & Nicolson 1985

J.E. Zeigler: "The Medieval Virgin as Object: Art of Anthropology?", *Historical Reflections*, XVI, 1989

Charles Zika: "Hosts, Processions and Pilgrimages: Controlling the Sacred in Fifteenth-Century Germany", *Past and Present*, CXVIII, 1988

CRESCENT MOON PUBLISHING

web: www.crmoon.com e-mail: cresmopub@yahoo.co.uk

ARTS, PAINTING, SCULPTURE

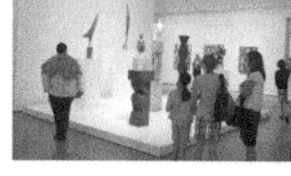
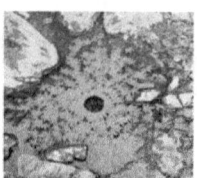
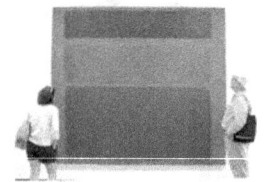

The Art of Andy Goldsworthy
Andy Goldsworthy: Touching Nature
Andy Goldsworthy in Close-Up
Andy Goldsworthy: Pocket Guide
Andy Goldsworthy In America
Land Art: A Complete Guide
The Art of Richard Long
Richard Long: Pocket Guide
Land Art In the UK
Land Art in Close-Up
Land Art In the U.S.A.
Land Art: Pocket Guide
Installation Art in Close-Up
Minimal Art and Artists In the 1960s and After
Colourfield Painting
Land Art DVD, TV documentary
Andy Goldsworthy DVD, TV documentary
The Erotic Object: Sexuality in Sculpture From Prehistory to the Present Day
Sex in Art: Pornography and Pleasure in Painting and Sculpture
Postwar Art
Sacred Gardens: The Garden in Myth, Religion and Art
Glorification: Religious Abstraction in Renaissance and 20th Century Art
Early Netherlandish Painting
Leonardo da Vinci
Piero della Francesca
Giovanni Bellini
Fra Angelico: Art and Religion in the Renaissance
Mark Rothko: The Art of Transcendence
Frank Stella: American Abstract Artist
Jasper Johns
Brice Marden
Alison Wilding: The Embrace of Sculpture
Vincent van Gogh: Visionary Landscapes
Eric Gill: Nuptials of God
Constantin Brancusi: Sculpting the Essence of Things
Max Beckmann
Caravaggio
Gustave Moreau
Egon Schiele: Sex and Death In Purple Stockings
Delizioso Fotografico Fervore: Works In Process 1
Sacro Cuore: Works In Process 2
The Light Eternal: J.M.W. Turner
The Madonna Glorified: Karen Arthurs

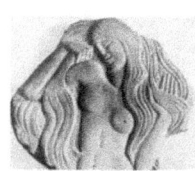
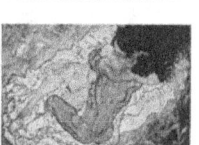
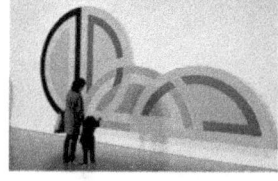
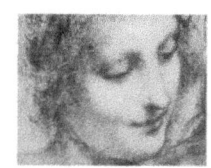
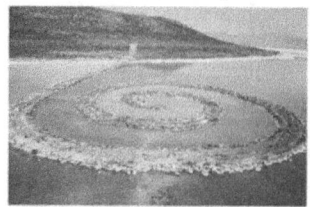

LITERATURE

J.R.R. Tolkien: The Books, The Films, The Whole Cultural Phenomenon
J.R.R. Tolkien: Pocket Guide
Tolkien's Heroic Quest
The *Earthsea* Books of Ursula Le Guin
Beauties, Beasts and Enchantment: Classic French Fairy Tales
German Popular Stories by the Brothers Grimm
Philip Pullman and *His Dark Materials*
Sexing Hardy: Thomas Hardy and Feminism
Thomas Hardy's *Tess of the d'Urbervilles*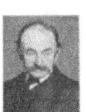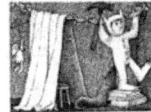
Thomas Hardy's *Jude the Obscure*
Thomas Hardy: The Tragic Novels
Love and Tragedy: Thomas Hardy
The Poetry of Landscape in Hardy
Wessex Revisited: Thomas Hardy and John Cowper Powys
Wolfgang Iser: Essays and Interviews
Petrarch, Dante and the Troubadours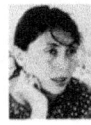
Maurice Sendak and the Art of Children's Book Illustration
Andrea Dworkin
Cixous, Irigaray, Kristeva: The *Jouissance* of French Feminism
Julia Kristeva: Art, Love, Melancholy, Philosophy, Semiotics and Psychoanalysis
Hélène Cixous I Love You: The *Jouissance* of Writing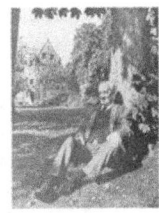
Luce Irigaray: Lips, Kissing, and the Politics of Sexual Difference
Peter Redgrove: Here Comes the Flood
Peter Redgrove: Sex-Magic-Poetry-Cornwall
Lawrence Durrell: Between Love and Death, East and West
Love, Culture & Poetry: Lawrence Durrell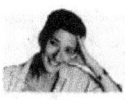
Cavafy: Anatomy of a Soul
German Romantic Poetry: Goethe, Novalis, Heine, Hölderlin
Feminism and Shakespeare
Shakespeare: Love, Poetry & Magic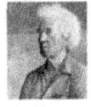
The Passion of D.H. Lawrence
D.H. Lawrence: Symbolic Landscapes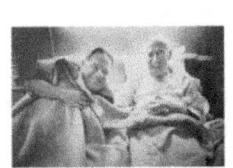
D.H. Lawrence: Infinite Sensual Violence
Rimbaud: Arthur Rimbaud and the Magic of Poetry
The Ecstasies of John Cowper Powys
Sensualism and Mythology: The Wessex Novels of John Cowper Powys
Amorous Life: John Cowper Powys and the Manifestation of Affectivity (H.W. Fawkner)
Postmodern Powys: New Essays on John Cowper Powys (Joe Boulter)
Rethinking Powys: Critical Essays on John Cowper Powys
Paul Bowles & Bernardo Bertolucci
Rainer Maria Rilke
Joseph Conrad: *Heart of Darkness*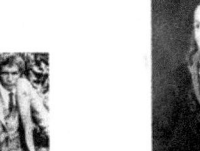
In the Dim Void: Samuel Beckett
Samuel Beckett Goes into the Silence
André Gide: Fiction and Fervour
Jackie Collins and the Blockbuster Novel
Blinded By Her Light: The Love-Poetry of Robert Graves
The Passion of Colours: Travels In Mediterranean Lands
Poetic Forms

POETRY

Ursula Le Guin: Walking In Cornwall
Peter Redgrove: Here Comes The Flood
Peter Redgrove: Sex-Magic-Poetry-Cornwall
Dante: Selections From the Vita Nuova
Petrarch, Dante and the Troubadours
William Shakespeare: Sonnets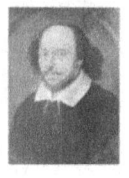
William Shakespeare: Complete Poems
Blinded By Her Light: The Love-Poetry of Robert Graves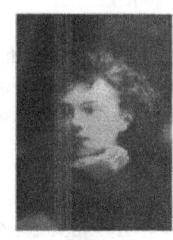
Emily Dickinson: Selected Poems
Emily Brontë: Poems
Thomas Hardy: Selected Poems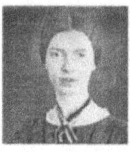
Percy Bysshe Shelley: Poems
John Keats: Selected Poems
Joh n Keats: Poems of 1820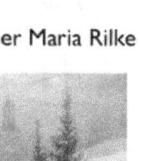
D.H. Lawrence: Selected Poems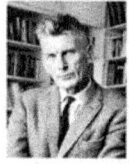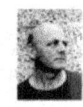
Edmund Spenser: Poems
Edmund Spenser: Amoretti
John Donne: Poems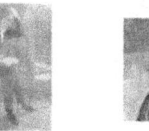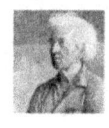
Henry Vaughan: Poems
Sir Thomas Wyatt: Poems
Robert Herrick: Selected Poems
Rilke: Space, Essence and Angels in the Poetry of Rainer Maria Rilke
Rainer Maria Rilke: Selected Poems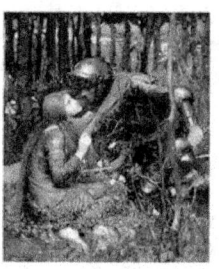
Friedrich Hölderlin: Selected Poems
Arseny Tarkovsky: Selected Poems
Arthur Rimbaud: Selected Poems
Arthur Rimbaud: A Season in Hell
Arthur Rimbaud and the Magic of Poetry
Novalis: Hymns To the Night
German Romantic Poetry
Paul Verlaine: Selected Poems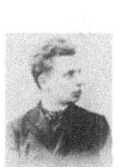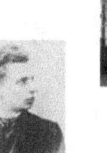
Elizaethan Sonnet Cycles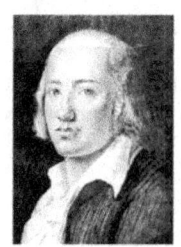
D.J. Enright: By-Blows
Jeremy Reed: Brigitte's Blue Heart
Jeremy Reed: Claudia Schiffer's Red Shoes
Gorgeous Little Orpheus
Radiance: New Poems
Crescent Moon Book of Nature Poetry
Crescent Moon Book of Love Poetry
Crescent Moon Book of Mystical Poetry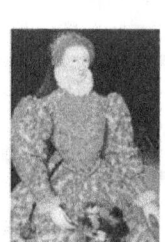
Crescent Moon Book of Elizabethan Love Poetry
Crescent Moon Book of Metaphysical Poetry
Crescent Moon Book of Romantic Poetry
Pagan America: New American Poetry

J.R.R. Tolkien: The Books, The Films, The Whole Cultural Phenomenon
J.R.R. Tolkien: Pocket Guide
The *Lord of the Rings* Movies: Pocket Guide
The Cinema of Hayao Miyazaki
Hayao Miyazaki: *Princess Mononoke*: Pocket Movie Guide
Hayao Miyazaki: *Spirited Away*: Pocket Movie Guide
Tim Burton : Hallowe'en For Hollywood
Ken Russell
Ken Russell: *Tommy*: Pocket Movie Guide
The Ghost Dance: The Origins of Religion
The Peyote Cult
Cixous, Irigaray, Kristeva: The *Jouissance* of French Feminism
Julia Kristeva: Art, Love, Melancholy, Philosophy, Semiotics and Psychoanalysis
Luce Irigaray: Lips, Kissing, and the Politics of Sexual Difference
Hélène Cixous I Love You: The *Jouissance* of Writing
Andrea Dworkin
'Cosmo Woman': The World of Women's Magazines
Women in Pop Music
HomeGround: The Kate Bush Anthology
Discovering the Goddess (Geoffrey Ashe)
The Poetry of Cinema
The Sacred Cinema of Andrei Tarkovsky
Andrei Tarkovsky: Pocket Guide
Andrei Tarkovsky: *Mirror*: Pocket Movie Guide
Andrei Tarkovsky: *The Sacrifice*: Pocket Movie Guide
Walerian Borowczyk: Cinema of Erotic Dreams
Jean-Luc Godard: The Passion of Cinema
Jean-Luc Godard: *Hail Mary*: Pocket Movie Guide
Jean-Luc Godard: *Contempt*: Pocket Movie Guide
Jean-Luc Godard: *Pierrot le Fou*: Pocket Movie Guide
John Hughes and Eighties Cinema
Ferris Bueller's Day Off: Pocket Movie Guide
Jean-Luc Godard: Pocket Guide
The Cinema of Richard Linklater
Liv Tyler: Star In Ascendance
Blade Runner and the Films of Philip K. Dick
Paul Bowles and Bernardo Bertolucci
Media Hell: Radio, TV and the Press
An Open Letter to the BBC
Detonation Britain: Nuclear War in the UK
Feminism and Shakespeare
Wild Zones: Pornography, Art and Feminism
Sex in Art: Pornography and Pleasure in Painting and Sculpture
Sexing Hardy: Thomas Hardy and Feminism

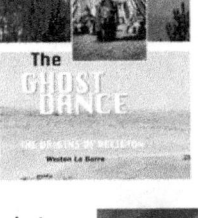
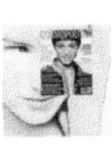
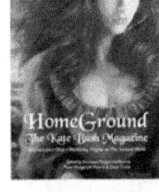
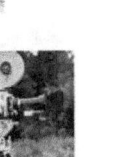
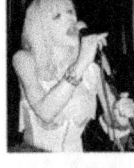
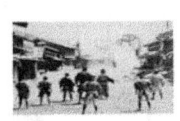
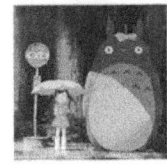
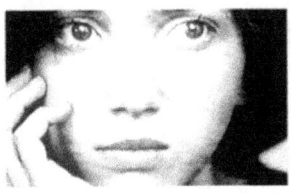

The Light Eternal is a model monograph, an exemplary job. The subject matter of the book is beautifully organised and dead on beam. (Lawrence Durrell)
It is amazing for me to see my work treated with such passion and respect. (Andrea Dworkin)

CRESCENT MOON PUBLISHING
P.O. Box 1312, Maidstone, Kent, ME14 5XU, Great Britain. www.crmoon.com

cresmopub@yahoo.co.uk   www.crescentmoon.org.uk

www.ingramcontent.com/pod-product-compliance
Lightning Source LLC
Chambersburg PA
CBHW072014230526
45468CB00021B/1461

www.ingramcontent.com/pod-product-compliance
Lightning Source LLC
Chambersburg PA
CBHW071244220526
45468CB00002B/992